BEARSTONE

with
CONNECTIONS

BEARSTONE

Will Hobbs

with
CONNECTIONS

HOLT, RINEHART AND **WINSTON**

Harcourt Brace & Company

Austin • New York • Orlando • Atlanta • San Francisco
Boston • Dallas • Toronto • London

For permission to reprint copyrighted material, grateful acknowledgment is made to the following sources:

Atheneum Books for Young Readers, Simon & Schuster Children's Publishing Division: *Bearstone* by Will Hobbs. Copyright © 1989 by Will Hobbs. All rights reserved.

Arte Público Press: "Lesson 1" and "Lesson 2" from *Chants* by Pat Mora. Copyright © 1985 by Pat Mora. Published by Arte Público Press – University of Houston, 1985. **Copper Canyon Press, P.O. Box 271, Port Townsend, WA 98368:** "the earth is a living thing" from *The Book of Light* by Lucille Clifton. Copyright © 1993 by Lucille Clifton. **Firebrand Books, Ithaca, New York:** "Dancer" from *Simple Songs* by Vickie Sears. Copyright © 1990 by Vickie Sears. **John Hawkins & Associates, Inc.:** "My Friend Flicka" by Mary O'Hara. Copyright © 1941 by Mary O'Hara. **Will Hobbs:** Comment on *Beardance* by Will Hobbs. Copyright © 1996 by Will Hobbs. **Harold Ober Associates:** From "Foreword," "In Africa," "The Name-Giver," "Rawautoaqvaywoaky," and "So You Changed Your Name?" from *A Book About Names* by Milton Meltzer. Copyright © 1984 by Milton Meltzer. **Philomel Books, a division of Penguin Putnam Inc.:** "Baby Bear Moon" from *Thirteen Moons on a Turtle's Back* by Joseph Bruchac and Jonathan Logan. Copyright © 1992 by Joseph Bruchac and Jonathan Logan. **Nancy Wood, c/o Frances Collin Literary Agency:** "Here on This Mountain" from *War Cry on a Prayer Feather: Prose and Poetry of the Ute Indians* by Nancy Wood. Copyright © 1979 by Nancy Wood.

Cover illustration: Higgins Bond/ American Artist Rep., Inc.

FOR JEAN

With special thanks to Greg, Ed, Dad, Joe, Dan, Jeff, Jean, Diane, Matt, Suzy, and Pepsi for all the Pine River memories. Thanks to Loyd for the inspiration and to Mike for the story of his ride through the Window.

Books by Will Hobbs

Contents

Cloyd stood a step from the door of the hospital room. His father was in that room. "Are you sure you have to see him in person to deliver those flowers?" the nurse asked.

"They won't pay me unless I deliver them in person."

Cloyd didn't think it would work if he told her who he was. He had run away from the Ute group home in Colorado and hitched all the way to Window Rock, Arizona, to find his father. That's where the Navajos kept the records about everyone in the whole tribe, and there he found out that yes, there was a Leeno Atcitty, and his address was listed as the Indian Health Service Hospital in Window Rock. He was a patient there.

Cloyd wondered how he might get into his father's hospital room to see him. If he told them who he was, there would be trouble because he had run away. Then he had an idea. He used the last of his money to buy some flowers.

For years Cloyd had been asking every Navajo he happened to meet if they knew a man named Leeno Atcitty. "What does he look like?" they'd ask. Cloyd couldn't tell them; he'd never known his father. He'd grown up without him, with only his sister and his grandmother. Cloyd knew just two things about his father—he was a Navajo, and he had disappeared after Cloyd was born. Nobody had seen him since.

When Cloyd was little, he used to talk to his sister about how badly he wanted to find his father, but she didn't seem to need to know him at all, so he had kept his dream inside. In the year since he'd been sent away, the more lonely he became, the stronger his desire grew to find his father. Now here he was with his heart pounding, following the nurse down the long hallway to his father's room.

The nurse stopped short of the door and said, "Why don't you let me take the flowers in."

Cloyd didn't know if this was going to work. He wasn't a good liar. He said, "I'm supposed to deliver them myself."

"I've never seen you here before. Who did you say you're working for?"

He knew he had to do something quick. Like a rabbit in the sagebrush, Cloyd was into the room.

What he saw terrified him. This wasn't even a human being. It was more like a shriveled-up mummy attached to a bunch of tubes. One went into his nose and one went into his arm. A third came out from under the sheet. How could this be his father? Was it even alive? "What's the matter with him?" he asked as evenly as he could.

"Have you ever heard of the expression 'brain dead'? It means his heart and his lungs still work, but his brain is . . . well, dead. I tried to tell you, it's not a pretty sight. He won't know about the flowers."

Cloyd had to keep talking, or the nurse would get onto him. He had to put away his terror, not show any emotion on his face. He was good at that. "How did this happen?"

"Car accident," she said. "I don't know any details."

"How long has he been like this?"

"Four years."

"Are you sure he's Leeno Atcitty?"

"Yes, of course."

"Where's he from?"

"I think I heard that once . . . Utah, I think. Monument Valley. I wonder if this could be the man you were looking for. Nobody ever sent him flowers before."

He knew it was his father. His father came from Monument Valley. Besides, the Navajos listed only one Leeno Atcitty.

Cloyd shrugged. "The people that ordered the flowers said he had a broken leg. Is there another Leeno Atcitty in the hospital?"

He sneaked one last look at his father. The terror returned full force. How could this . . . wrinkled, shrunken shell of a human being be his father? He

3

forgot to wait for her reply. He turned and left without looking back.

"No," she said after him. "I'm sure there isn't. . . . There must have been some mistake."

He threw the flowers in the trash.

2

Cloyd wanted to go home to Utah, back to White Mesa. Every mile took him farther into Colorado, farther even than Durango, where he'd spent the lonely winter in the group home. He was looking out the window of the van at the beaver dams in the creek along the highway. There weren't any beaver dams where he came from.

His housemother didn't speak, and he was glad. She'd said it all before. How he couldn't go home for the summer, how she'd had this idea to put him on a ranch with an old man whose wife had died, and how much he was going to like it.

What was the old man going to be like? Cloyd wished he didn't have to meet this Walter Landis. Why wouldn't these people just leave him alone? All winter in the group home, through the miserable days in school, he had looked forward to going home for the summer. Now even that was being taken away from him. They were afraid his grandmother wouldn't make him mind, that she'd let him disappear into the canyons again. Cloyd thought about how good that would be, to disappear and be free. He wanted to run away again, hitchhike home to White Mesa. When he was trying to find his father, he'd hitched all over.

"Getting close," his housemother announced cheerfully. She pulled off the highway onto a bumpy dirt road. "Look, there's the river, Cloyd—the Piedra River—through the trees!"

Cloyd had already noticed the river and the big pines. It was so different from the high desert back home. He rolled the window down all the way. It smelled like . . . pine cones.

"Walter's is the only place north of the highway," Susan James said. "After his place, it's all wilderness for a hundred miles and more."

Cloyd noticed how she drove slowly and deliberately through the potholes, slower than she would have had to. There was only a short time left before she dropped him off. Probably she was going to tell him to behave. This rancher was an old friend of hers. There, ahead, was the gate. Cloyd thought how much he didn't want to meet this stranger. He could hide and then hitch to Utah. He could visit his grandmother, at night when nobody would know. Then he would take off for the canyons. Nobody could find him in the canyons.

"Would you open the gate, Cloyd? Just look at that lovely orchard."

He got out of the van and opened the gate. Through the orchard he could see open fields, sheds, and a barn. Mostly hidden behind two blue spruce trees stood a gray two-story house. Somebody's home, not his. He could see a small figure stepping off the porch. Susan James was driving through the gate. Cloyd was supposed to close it behind her. He did, and then he bolted into the trees.

"Cloyd!" she called. "Cloyd, you come back here right now!"

He ran quickly and quietly. She was chasing him. Cloyd darted this way and that, then hid behind an enormous boulder. His heart was beating fast. He grinned; he knew she couldn't catch him. "For crying out loud," he heard her say.

Cloyd skittered twenty or more feet up the boulder's sloping backside, gained its nearly flat top, and lay on his belly. He heard her tramping around in the orchard and calling with her voice raised, thinking he was long gone. She was on her way back to the van when she and the old man met, not very far from the boulder. Cloyd could hear everything they said.

"So he's run off, has he, Susan?" the old man said. "And here I ain't even met him yet."

The voice sounded very old and very tired. Cloyd peeked over the edge and saw them talking. The old man's hands were in the pockets of his striped overalls, his shoulders were slumped, his bald head bowed. Purple veins stood out on his skull. The most surprising thing about him was his size. He was little. I'm taller and bigger than he is, Cloyd realized.

"Does he do that often—run away?" the old man asked.

7

"Only once before, and it sure got him in a whole lot of trouble. . . . I just thought being out here and working with you might be good for him. A chance with school out to get away from the group home where he's been getting into so much trouble. School has been a disaster for him."

"Oh? Well, I wasn't so good at school myself. . . ."

Cloyd saw his housemother frown. "I'll bet this is a lot worse than you ever did, Walter. He failed all seven of his classes. The school says he just won't do the work, but I'm not sure he even knows how. He's fourteen, but he missed four years of school back in Utah."

"Four years! Where was he?"

"Out in the canyons, herding his grandmother's goats. I think he's at least half-wild."

The old man grinned mischievously. "Now, ain't that somethin'."

Cloyd liked the old man's chuckle. The rancher didn't act like other grown-ups.

"So he was living with his grandmother?" Walter asked. "What about his parents—why isn't he with them?"

"His mother's dead—died when he was born. She was Ute. No one seems to know much about his father, just that he's a Navajo. He left when she died. Cloyd's always lived with his mother's people. So tell me about yourself, Walter. How've you been doing?"

"Not worth a darn. Since Maude passed away and I sold off the cows, I haven't even put up a hay crop."

"But look at these beautiful peaches," Susan James said brightly. "You can't tell me you're not taking care of this peach orchard."

"It's for her, Susan. . . for Maude. You know how she loved the peaches."

Cloyd peered into the thick green foliage. Until now, he hadn't noticed the trees around the boulder, he'd been so intent on listening. He was astonished. He never knew peach trees could grow so large, so full and lush, or set so much fruit. Peaches were treasured at White Mesa. He had always helped his grandmother harvest them, and it was a special time. But her trees couldn't begin to compare with these. He admired the rancher for owning these trees.

"Just look at all those baby peaches," Susan James said, pointing to branches loaded with fruit. "It amazes me that you can raise them here at all. I've never seen peaches at this altitude, much less in a canyon. Doesn't the cold air settle?"

The old man had that impish grin on his face again. "That's what makes it interesting."

"Do you still have that gold mine you always talked about? With the price of gold going up every day, you must be getting ideas."

The rancher sighed. "Oh, I've still got the Pride of the West, an' I still believe in her as much as ever, but I'm not so sure as I used to be that I'll ever get back there."

Cloyd turned onto his back and studied the cliffs high on the mountain above the river canyon. In reds and whites, the cliffs seemed like a huge chunk of the desert hovering over the forests. They reminded him of home. In a moment, he realized that the boulder underneath him made a perfect fit with a huge notch in the cliffs up above. It must have fallen long ago, leaving behind a shallow cave. He felt good about his insight. He wasn't stupid, like they thought. It was the first of June, a brilliant turquoise day, and he was out of school at last. He kind of liked the old rancher, too. I can hitchhike to Utah later, he thought. Anytime.

Sliding off the rock, Cloyd slipped through the orchard and vanished among the tall trees, then began to climb. He didn't know he was climbing toward a treasure and a turning point. He wanted only to reach that piece of desert in the sky.

3

Under the cover of the big pines, Cloyd climbed the steep slope in leaps. As he climbed, the ranch buildings shrank until only their shiny metal roofs showed, and the peach orchard looked like a bright green circle with a sandy center. A herd of horses appeared in a pasture by the river. He was pleased to see that the old man had horses. He used to have a horse once.

Cloyd let his thoughts take him back to White Mesa, as they had all winter. Almost a year away from his grandmother and his sister, he'd had to live at White Mesa in his mind or wither away and become nobody. All winter in Durango as Cloyd sat in one classroom, then passed like a sleepwalker at the bell to the next, his spirit roamed the canyons with the flock. He put out of his mind now his other dream, the one he used to live for, the one that had turned into the man in the hospital bed in Window Rock. White Mesa was his whole world now.

Finally he stood atop the red-and-white sandstone cliffs. They had the same feel as the cliffs in the canyons where he used to take the goats. But he'd never seen a view like this one. This was a shining new world. To the north and east, peaks still covered with snow shone in the cloudless blue sky. He'd never seen mountains so sharp and rugged, so fierce and splendid. Below him, an eagle soared high above the old man's field. It was a good sign.

Then he remembered his grandmother's parting words as he left for Colorado. She told him something he'd never heard before: their band of Weminuche Utes hadn't always lived at White Mesa. Colorado, especially the mountains above Durango, had been their home until gold was discovered there and the white men wanted them out of the way. Summers the people used to hunt and fish in the high mountains, she'd said; they knew every stream, places so out of the way that white men still hadn't seen them. "So don't feel bad about going to Durango," she told him.

Cloyd regarded the distant peaks with new strength, a fierce kind of pride he'd never felt before. These were the mountains where his people used to live. Maybe he should stay at the ranch. Maybe he could follow the river all the way up to those peaks and stand atop the highest one. If he worked hard, there would be time off. Maybe the old man would let him take one of his horses.

Tucked under a high ridge, the outcrop suddenly lost the sun. He should be returning to the ranch. He wondered if his housemother had driven back to Durango with his duffel bag. Halfway down the side of the cliffs, he discovered a ledge that might lead across them. That's what he liked to do back in the canyon country: follow ledges across cliffs. You never knew what you might find. This one led to that shadowy cave, the notch he'd seen from the orchard. Its high, arching roof was indeed the perfect match to the backside of the boulder he'd climbed among the peach trees.

Cloyd sprang to the ledge. If he was careful, he could follow it, at least for a way. Below him the cliff fell more than a hundred feet. There was no good reason he had to get to the cave, yet he knew he would try it. The place itself was driving him on. The cliff houses in the canyons used to exert the same pull on him. He'd managed those climbs, nearly as difficult as this one, by using the natural cracks in the canyon walls and the handholds the Ancient Ones had carved. And he'd stood many times in their ancient homes like nests, which were said to be unreachable without ladders. When he reached those places, he felt good, standing alone in a good place.

The ledge narrowed to a seam. Arms spread wide, fingers splayed on the sandstone, Cloyd started across it with his face to the cliff wall. Carefully he edged sideways on the tips of his toes with his right foot gingerly exploring, then choosing new footing, the left following after, until he was nearly there. With a swoon he realized he could no longer lean into the cliff. The shape of the rock had forced his body weight out over thin air, and he was in bad trouble. Stretched tight, the tendons above his heels began to quiver, then to tremble. His strength deserted him in a rush. He paused to rest, but his legs began to shake violently.

His fingers started to go numb. He fought the panic and tried to think. He knew he had to go forward, reach the cave, and rest. He'd never make it back unless he could rest.

Cloyd breathed deeply and summoned a little strength into his legs. He started out again, more quickly than before. Shuffling the last few steps, he fell gasping onto the chalky floor of the cave.

Once he caught his breath, Cloyd looked for what he might find. It would take his mind off the return across the cliff. If this cave were back in the canyon country, he thought, it would have a ruin in it and maybe some picture writing. But it was bowl-smooth and empty, except for a large fin of sandstone broken loose from the wall and ceiling. He noticed something wedged between the wall and the fin—a shape that didn't look quite natural. He shimmied into the dark, narrow crack until his hands closed on some kind of a bundle, and then he backed out into the light to see what it was.

He knelt and examined it up close. He probed with his fingers. Turkey feathers and fur, probably rabbit: hundreds of tiny bits of feather and fur wrapped around cords of yucca fiber. A blanket, a whole blanket in the style of the Ancient Ones.

Carefully he folded the blanket back and gasped to see a very small human face with empty eye sockets. The brown skin and black hair were still intact. At once he knew he was holding a burial in his hands, one of the Ancient Ones. His grandmother talked about such things, but he'd never seen one in all his time in the canyons. Her advice came to mind: behave carefully, treat the buried one with the utmost respect, and don't make any mistakes. The Ancient Ones are not people to be trifled with.

An infant, he realized. Buried in the position his grandmother had described, with the legs folded and tucked against the stomach. The best thing to do was think a good intention and return it to its resting place.

When Cloyd wriggled back with the bundle to the place where he'd found it, he saw the silhouette of a piece of pottery, a jar with handles and a short, slender neck. He brought it into the open where he could see it, and took in its beauty and wholeness. Before this he'd found countless shards with similar black-lined designs, but never anything close to a whole pot. It was said they were worth a thousand dollars unbroken.

As he turned the pot on its side to admire it, something moved inside. He let the loose object fall gently into his hand. His heart leaped to see a small blue stone about two inches long, worn smooth by long handling. Turquoise. Two eyes, a snout, and a humped back. A bear. Surely, a bear to accompany the infant on the long journey.

His grandmother had told him about bears. The most important of all animals to the Utes, she'd said— friend and relative of man, bringer of strength and luck. If you could make a bear your personal guardian, you would be a strong man and lucky. In the old days, she said, when the people lived side by side with the bears, they would not kill them. That would bring on themselves the worst of bad luck.

Cloyd turned the smooth blue stone in his hand. He felt he was meant to cross the cliff and find this stone. He had earned this bear-stone; his grandmother would understand. She was the only person he knew who remembered the old ways and believed in their power. He'd always wondered if there was anything to her tales. Now he was sure there was. With this token, he felt like a new and powerful person.

His grandmother had said that in the old days, people had a secret name that was known only to one other person—a name that described who they really were, not who the world thought they were. He had thought he would like to have such a name for himself, but this naming was no longer done. "I'll take a name for myself," he thought, eyeing the stone in his hand. "I don't need a father; I don't need anyone." Then he said aloud, "My name is Lone Bear."

Cloyd returned the jar to the Ancient One. He tried to talk to the infant in his mind, told it that it must have reached its destination by now, and please, he'd like to have the stone on his own life's journey because he, Lone Bear, had great need of the strength and good luck it would bring.

Cloyd put the smooth stone in his pocket and started back across the precipice. This time his legs did not shake. His feet were sure, and his fingers exerted a powerful grip on the face of the cliff.

He raced down the mountain in the twilight, slowing his descent by clinging for moments to branches as he flew by them. With the bear in his pocket, he wasn't afraid of the oncoming darkness. In an odd sort of way, he was looking forward to seeing the curious old man at the ranch. Maybe the summer job wouldn't be so bad after all. Maybe he could follow the river to the high peaks.

At any rate, he had the bearstone. He kept checking his pocket to make sure it was still there.

4

It was dark. Walter tried to read his latest *Mining Gazette* in the parlor but couldn't concentrate for worrying about the teenager. He might've run off, but he might've slipped into the river. Swift and cold, the Piedra had drowned more than a few. He went outside, called the boy's name, and listened, but all he could hear was the river. Before too long he'd have to phone Susan James. He was supposed to call if Cloyd didn't show up.

Walter went inside and turned the heat down on the breaded pork chops he'd fixed. Since his wife died, he hadn't eaten regular meals. He'd eat a little of this and that, mostly from the canned goods in the basement. Old friends who dropped by would admonish him for not keeping up his strength, but as he told them, he was never hungry. With the boy coming, he'd had to get into town, do some shopping, plan some meals, and start thinking about how to cook them. He thought he'd take his flashlight downstream and look along the riverbank. In the mudroom closet Walter collected his wool coat and sat down on the bench to pull on his rubber boots. Two soft knocks sounded on the door. "Come on in," he said.

The boy stepped inside, avoiding Walter's eyes. Walter noticed the jeans first, wet from the knees down, then the fresh mud on the sneakers. The boy had gotten wet only minutes before, and not in the river. Crossing the irrigation ditch, Walter realized. Then he saw the T-shirt, with a fishhook-shaped rip across the belly. The shirt was badly soiled, yet white enough to accent the darkness of Cloyd's face and arms, which were the deepest shade of brown. His limbs were rounded, undefined, and he was chunky overall in the way of Ute men. Shiny black hair hung straight to his shoulders. Cloyd's large, round face was devoid of expression, unless it was the mouth turning dourly down at the corners. A bloody scratch shone bright red against his dark brown cheek.

"Got some supper here," Walter said. "You like pork chops?"

Cloyd shrugged. "Okay, I guess."

Walter put away the coat and flashlight, thinking he'd best not embarrass the boy by mentioning his clothes or the scratches. But he wouldn't have the boy tracking through the house in muddy sneakers. "I like to leave my outside shoes here in this mudroom," he said over his shoulder as he left.

Cloyd joined him in the kitchen in wet socks. "I put

your stuff up in your room," Walter said. "That's upstairs. The stairs are just off the parlor, and the bathroom is off the backside of the kitchen—that closed door over there. Would you like to shower and change clothes, or eat right away?"

"I'm hungry," Cloyd said softly.

Walter caught the black eyes darting toward him, then quickly away. "That'd be fine. Why, I'm hungry myself."

They ate quietly. Cloyd liked that. The old man wasn't all over him with questions. He looked around. The old man had an old-fashioned cookstove alongside the modern one. The cookstove was much like his grandmother's, only this one had bright blue enamel, where hers was all black and rusted in places. "You like that kind of stove?" he asked suddenly, pointing with a twist of the lips, as he finished up the food on his plate.

"Sure do. Still cook on it some, but mostly we used it for heating this side of the house in the winter. You can't beat them old stoves. Say, whyn't you have another go-round?" he said, indicating the pork chops and potatoes left on the platter. "Help yourself."

Cloyd shook his head. He felt freer refusing food.

"No? Make a good snack for tomorrow, then. But hang on. I've got something special to bring up from the basement for dessert."

On the old man's return, Cloyd sneaked a look at him. He sure was little. And he was really happy about his peaches—he had a big smile on his face and he carried the quart jar like it was a treasure.

"Like some?" Walter said with his grin.

Cloyd wasn't going to refuse this time; he nodded

enthusiastically. These peaches were large as store-bought. He loved peaches. He allowed the old man to dish up two large scoops of vanilla ice cream with the fruit.

The old man dished himself up some peaches and joined him.

"We have peaches at home, too," Cloyd said. "Not as big as yours."

"Size don't matter. That's pretty country, Utah is. Any canyons where you come from?"

"All over," Cloyd said. "Lots of ruins . . . from the Ancient Ones."

"Cliff dwellers? Like at Mesa Verde? Now ain't that somethin'."

Cloyd was curious. He had to ask. "Any ruins around here?" he asked carefully.

"Well, up on Chimney Rock Mesa, down the river a few miles and up the other side."

"I mean real close."

"Well, they say they lived all along the river—I've found a few grinding stones and whatnot, a few ar-rowheads and some potsherds. . . ."

Cloyd felt the stone in his pocket. He almost wanted to tell, but he knew he shouldn't. It was his secret. It had to do with his secret name.

"So you had a look around today, did you . . . Cloyd?" the old man asked awkwardly.

Cloyd wanted to tell at least some of the truth. "I climbed up above the cliff," he said.

Walter perked up. "Why, that's one of my favorite places around the farm. I used to climb up there my-self. Haven't for a good while, though."

"How come you call it a *farm*? This place is a *ranch*."

"Well, my wife came from farm country in Missouri, and she always said a ranch was like a house, but a farm was a home."

Cloyd finished the last of the syrup from the jar. He wasn't hungry anymore.

As he went upstairs, Cloyd noticed the picture of the old man's wife. It was on top of the bookcase by the stairs. He tried to imagine the white-haired woman with the friendly smile saying to the old man, "A ranch is like a house, but a farm is a home." He thought about what it meant as he looked around his room, unpacked his things from his duffel bag, then lay down on the bed with the bearstone in the palm of his hand. This was a good place, Walter's farm.

5

Walter knocked early on Cloyd's door. Cloyd woke to a warm house cheerful with the smell of sausage and eggs. Walter had fired up the cookstove and cooked breakfast on it. Cloyd ate with an eye on the fire showing through the draft slot. The old man opened the warmer door by the stovepipe and brought out sweet rolls.

"My grandmother keeps the frybread warm in there," Cloyd said.

"She raised you, didn't she?"

Cloyd nodded. He was beginning to feel uncomfortable. It sounded like Walter knew about his mother, how she died getting him born, how his father had run off. Walter wouldn't know what had happened to his father. He was the only one who knew that, and he wasn't going to tell anybody, not even his sister or grandmother.

"Where does your sister live?" Walter asked gently.

"Salt Lake. She goes to a boarding school. I haven't seen her for a long time."

"That's too bad."

Cloyd felt more uncomfortable. He didn't want any pity. He wanted to talk about something else. "What are my jobs?" he asked.

The old man stroked the white stubble on his chin. "What needs doing worst around here is the foundation wall down in the basement. It has a bad crack in it. I don't know about you, but summer's no time to work indoors to my way of thinking, so I'm gonna put that one off. Irrigating the hayfields will keep me plenty busy, so I want to find you a project you can work on your own at. I've got something in mind, but I need to chew on it a little longer. Let's take a look around while I think about it—I'm just getting the hang of things myself after lettin' the farm set last year."

They went outside. Cloyd followed Walter up the stairway inside the big red barn. The loft upstairs was huge, and empty except for a dozen or so bales of hay off in one corner. Swallows were flying in and out by the hundreds. There were nests everywhere with baby birds.

"Sure feels empty, don't it?" Walter remarked. "I used to fill all this up with hay—fed a lot of cows. You see, Cloyd, I didn't hardly hit a lick last summer."

"How come?"

"On account of losing my wife. Hit me awful hard.

24

Thought I didn't have anything to live for, to tell you the truth."

Cloyd didn't know what to say. He pointed with his lips to the meager haystack. "You don't have enough for your horses . . . for the winter."

"Oh, you saw the horses then. Yes, sir, it's time I baled some hay. Pretty soon the fields'll run to foxtails if I don't, and then they won't be worth a darn to anybody."

"Did you ever have any kids?"

"No, never did," he said softly. "We'd of liked to, but it just never happened." There was a long silence, and Cloyd regretted the question.

"Say, I've got something I want to show you," Walter announced, and led Cloyd downstairs to the tack room.

Everywhere Cloyd looked were saddles and bridles and gear he didn't even know what to call. It was a wealth of leather, and he liked the smell of it. "I always used to ride bareback . . . ." he said cautiously. "I don't know anything about this stuff."

Walter beamed. "I could sure show you. If you'd like to ride, you could take your pick of the horses. Most are packhorses, but there's a few good saddle horses among em, and they need riding—I can't seem to find the time."

"What are packhorses?"

"Why, they're for carryin' loads—into the mountains, where there's no roads."

The mountains, Cloyd thought. He's all set up for the mountains. He's got the gear and the horses, and maybe he would take me. . . . "Do you go to the mountains?"

"That's a long story. . . . I've been keepin' horses for years, thinkin' I was going to get back up there and reopen a mine I've got up in the high country."

"You like mining?"

A big smile lit the old man's face. "You bet I do."

"What do you like about it?"

"Why, the gold, I suppose. Sounds crazy, but the price of gold yesterday was four hundred fifty-six dollars an *ounce*. When I was minin', gold was around thirty-two dollars. Makes a difference, don't it?"

"How come you quit if you liked it?"

"I got married, Cloyd. My wife made me promise to give it up."

The old man lowered his voice. "She was scared to death of mines, thinkin' they're cavin' in all the time. But what she never understood was that the Pride of the West won't cave in—never. I used to tell her it was safer than this house. There's not a stick of timberwork in that whole mine—it's a hard-rock gold mine if ever there was one. But now, back to the horses . . . how'd you like to look 'em over? We could take a feed bag and a halter up to the pasture and you could pick one out. I'm going to do some irrigating later, but you could—"

Cloyd shook his head. "What about my job?"

"We could line that out tomorrow. I want to see what you think of these horses."

They each had a feed bag and a halter. They found the horses in the shade of the big pines along the river upstream. There were ten of them. "They'll be pretty skittish," Walter said. "Haven't been rode."

Cloyd knew immediately which one he wanted: the blue roan, a big, well-muscled gelding. White hairs intermingled with gray underneath gave the roan a blue tinge all over. He wanted to call the horse to him, but he felt embarrassed having the old man see him. What if the horse wouldn't come? He had to try. "Hey—a, hey—a," Cloyd called softly. "Hey—a, hey—a." While the others shied away, the big roan came to him, slowly and alertly, its head held high to one side. Its nostrils flared as it caught the scent of the grain. Cloyd let the horse almost finish the grain before he slipped the halter over its head.

"Nice," Walter said. "Very nice. You made that look easy. I'm partial to that sorrel mare yonder—got a real easy gait."

They led the two horses back to the barn. Cloyd admired the roan's lines, the way it carried itself. At every moment it seemed about to bolt, yet never did. The horse wasn't giving up its freedom, he thought. We chose each other.

First they curried the horses, then Walter showed him all about how to bridle and saddle his horse. The old man talked slow and made it easy to understand. "This blue roan's a smart'un. See how he puffs out his gut so you won't cinch him tight? And then the saddle falls off later and you with it."

Cloyd laughed. "Better not let him hear you. . . ."

"He thinks he's fooled us," Walter whispered. He turned away as if he was done, then winked and quickly cinched in a few more notches. "I wasn't born yesterday," he said.

Outside, Walter coached him on how to mount the

big roan. "Confidence is the main thing. He's gonna be skittish—been too long since he had a man on his back. One quick move, and don't quit halfway. Let him feel your confidence."

As excited as he was, Cloyd calmed himself. He tried to talk to the big roan with his heart. You and me, blue horse, he thought. You're the most beautiful horse I've ever seen. I bet you can run fast. We'll be friends, you and me.

In one motion, much the way he used to when he rode bareback, he swung up into the saddle. The big roan lifted his head and took a step or two, then settled right down. Cloyd patted him on the neck.

"Well, I'll be," Walter chuckled. "He really took a shine to you. That horse never gave me the time of day."

"Does he have a name?"

"Never got around to it. None of 'em do."

They rode up the river trail through the big pines alongside the rapids. They followed the river for many miles, until the trail left it and climbed more than a thousand feet. The horse was surefooted and enjoyed the work. Cloyd was thrilled with the feel of the horse. He liked riding with the old man. He liked the wind in the trees and the gray jays and the way he felt. He hadn't felt this good in a long time. Finally he caught a glimpse of the river again, all white, in a gorge so deep and narrow it stirred his heart to beating loud. Like thousands of knives, the dark walls were flinty and jagged, so unlike the smooth sandstones of home. Cloyd remembered the snowy peaks he'd seen towering over the mountains. This gorge, he realized, was only the beginning of that higher country. He took the blue stone from his pocket and turned it slowly in his hand. Someday, he vowed, he'd see those peaks up close. He would see the home of the Utes.

The sun was dropping fast. They had to turn around and head back for the farm. He did a lot of thinking on the way. He would work hard for the old man, harder than the old man could ever have dreamed, and then he would ask the old man to take him to the mountains.

"Blueboy," he whispered, naming the horse. "You and me, Blue. We'll get to the mountains. Blueboy and Lone Bear."

It was dusk. They were back down on river level, not far from the farm. Blueboy reared, and then Cloyd saw a black form ahead lope across the trail with an unusual gait, followed by another, smaller black shape. "A bear!" he said, his voice filled with amazement. "A bear with a cub, isn't it?"

"Black bear," Walter said. "Sure enough."

"I've never seen one before. There aren't any bears back home."

"Somethin' else, ain't they? They live here, sure enough, but you don't see 'em that often. Born for the wild."

6

Cloyd woke feeling good all over. As he yawned and stretched himself awake, he remembered his fleeting glimpse of the bear and the cub. What an amazing sight they were, he thought, and how lucky he'd been to see them. Or was it luck? He took the bearstone from under the pillow and turned it in his fingers. Lone Bear, he thought, that's the name I gave myself. These things were too wonderful to be accidents. His grandmother would understand. He recalled the feel of the powerful roan under him, and he heard the music in the old man's chuckle. He felt good, he felt strong. Now he wanted to prove himself.

"What's that job you were going to tell me about?" Cloyd asked at breakfast.

"Well, I'll need your help come haying time, bucking bales and putting up the hay, but of course that won't be until July. But I do have a project you could make a start on for me—I've been putting it off for a couple years now. Need to build a fence. I'm so busy irrigating the field, haying, fixing tractors and whatnot, I can't seem to get around to it."

"Show me about the fence. I can do that."

After breakfast, Cloyd followed Walter to a shed, where Walter picked out a posthole digger and a long steel bar. Cloyd grabbed the bar. It was six feet long and heavy, and he thought he could carry it better than the old man could. They walked through the lower field to the peach orchard and Walter's property line beyond it.

Walter set the tools down on the riverbank and led Cloyd along his line of short wooden survey stakes, one for each posthole that had to be dug, all the way across the end of the field from the river to the distant ditchbank at the base of the mountain. Then they walked back to the starting point. "What's this fence for?" Cloyd asked.

Walter's face went red suddenly as he looked away. Cloyd watched him closely.

"Well, Cloyd, I need to fence off a fellow that's been takin' advantage of me. This fellow—lives across the highway—he moves in from California a few years ago, buys himself a farm, and starts going broke, because he's no kind of farmer and won't listen if you try to help him, so he gets the idea he'll set himself up as a big-game guide—"

The old man ran short of breath, sputtered. Veins stood out on his forehead.

"He advertises in the big-city newspapers in Texas

like he's an outfitter, which he ain't licensed for, then he drives his hunters across my place in their four-wheel drives, tearin' up the field so bad you can't hay for the ruts. I only drive on the field myself when it's bone-dry. Then they park their trucks and horsetrailers right by the headgate where the trail takes out. He tells them I live on a county road with public access! The sheriff and the game warden, they've warned this fellow, but come fall he'll try it again. The sheriff says what I really need is a fence to go with my gate, and I guess he's right."

Walter's color returned, his breathing came easier. "You see, Cloyd, I've got the only access to a big piece of country up the Piedra here. There's no gov'ment trailhead anywhere near. So to get up the river to public land, folks have always had to come through my place. I don't mind when they ask beforehand and park downriver and walk or ride through, but this fellow doesn't know the meaning of courtesy. He's only out for himself."

Cloyd had watched with interest as Walter's anger rose. He could picture the neighbor from the other side of the highway driving up in the fall with his hunters and finding a new fence and a locked gate. The man would get out of his truck, walk along the fenceline, and see there was no way to get around it. Then he would have to turn around, and Walter would have won.

"Of course it's a two-year project, anyway," Walter said. "But we can make a start."

"I could finish this fence," Cloyd insisted.

"I don't think so. There's a lot of work in a fence like that. First off, since it's river bottom, you'll run into rocks sometimes, and to go deep enough to hold a post you'll have to break the rock with that bar and pull it out in pieces. Then there's all the posts to log out of the woods, wire to run—there's a lot of work in it. You'll be a help to me if you get some of the holes dug."

Walter dug the first hole to get Cloyd started. "No rocks in this'un," he said. "Lucked out."

Cloyd took the posthole digger from the old man, pulled out the next stake, and started to dig.

"Say," Walter said, "Whyn't you hold off until I can fetch a pair of gloves for you and a jug of ice water. And a cap, too. I always wear one when I'm standin' out in the sun irrigatin'."

"I never wear a hat."

"There probably won't be much cloud cover until later in the month . . . usually doesn't start raining until the Fourth of July."

Cloyd shook his head. "I don't like hats."

"Suit yourself," Walter answered cheerfully. "Well, I better let the water into the field, or the grass is gonna burn up."

Cloyd let the old man disappear through the orchard, then started digging with all of his strength and determination. If he was going to get finished, he'd better get started. He could tell Walter had already forgotten he was going to bring back some gloves, but it didn't matter. He didn't like to use gloves.

The June days and Cloyd's line of completed postholes advanced steadily. His blisters healed, his hands grew callused. The white stubble on the old man's face lengthened into thick white whiskers. He said he was having a lark: he had never grown a beard in his whole life, and now he was going to. Cloyd liked the way it made him look. Like an old miner. He would look perfect, Cloyd thought, with a pick over his shoulder and leading a donkey.

Even though he didn't work with Walter during the day, Cloyd wasn't lonely. His mind was brimful of thinking as he worked the rhythm of the posthole digger. He thought about Blueboy and where they would ride that evening, and wondered if he would see another bear. The mountains he thought about, too, all the time. He'd made a promise to himself not to mention his plans to Walter until he had the fence finished, until he had proven himself, until he'd earned the mountains.

Every so often the blades of his posthole digger would strike a rock, and then Cloyd was in for a battle. First he'd try to dig another hole, but often he'd strike the same rock. Then there was no choice but to break it with the bar, and he would slam the bar down with all his might. He found a fierce satisfaction in breaking rock. And he knew the sound carried up to Walter in the field. The old man was surprised with how hard he could work and how many holes he had dug. Cloyd had never worked this hard before; he was surprising himself. In the early afternoon Walter would ring the porch bell, and they would eat a big meal. Then he'd go back to his postholes and work until Walter called him for supper.

In the evenings Cloyd would hurry out to saddle up the roan and take him for a ride. Blueboy could run like anything. The horse liked him, and he knew it. Cloyd felt good streaming along the river road with the wind in his hair. He talked to the horse all the time. The horse was the only one who knew his secret name and his secret plans.

Late in the evenings, Walter would read his mining journals. Cloyd liked to ask him what it was like in the high country. "Tell me about the mountains up real high," he'd say, "like where your mine is."

Walter would stroke his whiskers. "Oh, there's nothin' like it. Most beautiful country I've ever seen."

"Is there much water?"

"Oh, there's water everywhere. Little trickles runnin' off snowbanks, ponds, lakes, creeks, streams, baby rivers. . . . Some places the ground's so wet it's like walkin' on a sponge. It's as green as can be, and there's wildflowers everywhere you look."

"How high are the tops of the mountains?"

"Punch holes in the sky."

"Can you climb to the top?"

"If you got wings."

"What happens to the animals when winter comes?"

"Freeze solid," said the old man, with his tongue in his cheek. "Wouldn't you?"

It was a good time, talking about the mountains in the parlor. Walter would set his mining journal aside, the tiredness would leave his eyes, and a faraway look would come over him as he spoke. Cloyd liked to see him scratch his whiskers. He liked this old man, Walter Landis.

7

The days were scorching. Weeks passed with no cloud cover at all. Cloyd kept working. The shade of the nearby timber beckoned, but he resisted. He was getting closer all the time to digging that last posthole. In the evenings he'd sneak looks at the calendar; he kept trying to guess how long it would take him to build the fence. Day by day he was realizing it was a much bigger project than he'd thought at first, just as the old man had said.

Sundays were something to look forward to, the only break in the routine. Walter would go into Durango for groceries and supplies, and Cloyd would spend the day with Blueboy.

At breakfast, Walter was all dressed up for town and working on a shopping list. It was another Sunday, but Cloyd wasn't feeling very good about it. He woke up feeling bad, and he didn't know why. He only knew he wasn't very happy.

They hardly spoke over breakfast. The talk between them was dying out little by little. There was only the work.

He knew Walter could tell he was feeling bad. The old man was a long time buttering his toast. At last he said, trying to sound cheerful, "Gonna take Blueboy out today, Cloyd?"

Cloyd shrugged.

"I sure hope so. Say, I've been wondering if you might like to give that fenceline a rest. Maybe do a little of this and a little of that, take some more time with the horse."

"I don't want to," Cloyd said stubbornly.

Walter left for Durango. Cloyd knew he didn't want to ride Blueboy. He didn't feel good enough. There was a little flame of anger in him that was starting to grow. The old man was saying he should give up. Walter didn't really expect anything from him. Walter had heard all about school, how he'd failed everything. Now Walter expected him to fail here too. Well, they were all wrong about him, wrong to say he was lazy. He wanted to show the old man.

Cloyd shouldered the posthole digger and dragged the bar along behind. He didn't have that many holes to go. He wanted to get the posts in the ground before Walter needed his help with the hay. Then that would leave only stringing the wire.

Concentrating on his welding, Walter was startled to notice Cloyd standing beside him. Removing his mask, Walter switched off the arc welder. "How's it going, Cloyd?" he asked cheerfully.

"I finished those holes."

Walter beamed. "Well, Cloyd, that's downright amazin', is what it is. I never seen the like."

"We should finish the fence. So you'll have it before hunting season."

"I'd sure like to see it finished, too, Cloyd, but there's a lot of work left in it, fallin' junipers for posts and whatnot."

"I can start cutting the posts tomorrow."

The old man cast his eyes to the ground, removed his cap, ran his hand slowly over the top of his head and back. "Cloyd," he said finally, "I wish you'd let me cut the posts. After we get the hay in and it gets to rainin', I won't have to irrigate so much. I'll take out some junipers on the hill, clean 'em up so you can set 'em, then we'll string the wire together."

"You don't think I can do this job?"

"It's the chain saw I'm worried about. They're dangerous, Cloyd. I've used one for years, and I'm still scared of it. You see, sometimes a tree has a mind of its own, and there's plenty of ways you can make a mistake. Have you ever handled one?"

"You can show me," Cloyd insisted.

Walter saw how much it meant. At last he had to say, "Cloyd, I believe you can do just about anything you set your mind to."

Cloyd felt good as he walked up the field through the glowing late light to the barn. He took the bearstone out and turned it in his fingers, held it against his cheek. There was just enough evening left for him to visit the roan. "Hey-a, hey-a, " he called, and the horse nickered back.

The roan was waiting by the pasture gate. Cloyd fed him a little grain and then curried him, thinking aloud all the while. "You and me, Blue, we're gonna go to the mountains. I'm gonna finish it, finish everything; then we can go to the mountains, you and me."

In the morning Walter poked around the machine shed and collected the saw, an axe, a plastic bottle of bar-and-chain oil, a pint can of engine oil, an empty gas can, and a leather bag of tools. He told Cloyd all about the saw, and it seemed to Cloyd to take forever. Two or three times Walter cautioned Cloyd to mix the engine oil in with gas. "Straight gas'll ruin her, " he said. Cloyd didn't ask questions, and Walter didn't ask if he understood.

Walter knew the Utes weren't big talkers. He'd lived his whole life near the Colorado Utes, and his occasional contacts with them had taught him how to take things. The way Cloyd pointed with his lips-- only the old Utes did that anymore, something about it being rude to point with the hand or finger. And like the old-time Utes, Cloyd looked away when he talked or was spoken to.

Yet for all the time they'd spent together, Walter wished he understood Cloyd better. In the evenings Cloyd no longer asked about the mountains; he was bone-weary from working too hard. The boy would fall asleep watching the television. He himself was tiring, too, even questioning the need to set the farm back to rights. He was back to the old routines again, standing in the hot sun all day long and tediously

moving dirt and routing water. And Cloyd was working relentlessly, harder every day, for reasons of his
own. To whatever end, their course was set. Cloyd
couldn't be turned now. The only time he'd take for
himself was a short visit mornings and evenings with
the big roan. He'd work the currycomb and talk, talk,
talk with the horse. If I could inverview that horse,
Walter mused, I'd know the boy a whole lot better.

Cloyd thought it would take only a few days to log
out the posts he needed. He soon found out it wasn't
going to be that easy. The junipers grew only here
and there on the mountain. He wished he could use
the jack pines or the straight young firs. But
he knew why the old man wanted junipers—they'd
never rot.

He had to range the hillside the length of the farm,
hundreds of feet up the slope, to find his trees. If
anything, the work was harder than digging the
postholes. The saw was heavy and noisy; his ears were
always ringing. He burned his thumb on the exhaust
and cut the heel of his hand sharpening the chain.
After he felled a juniper, he had to top it to a seven-
foot length, trim it, then drag it down the hillside to
the ditch. The heavy posts often snagged in the oakbrush and brought him tumbling down. Even though
he had only fifty-seven posts cut, he knew he had to
get off the hillside for a while. He decided to set the
posts he had.

Placing a rock at the bottom of each hole the way
the old man had suggested, Cloyd set the posts. He
kept his eye on the tractor up the field as the old man
drove around cutting the hay. Walter would need his

help in a few days to buck the bales onto the trailer and stack them in the barn.

Cloyd set the fifty-seventh post as the sun was setting on the next-to-last day of June. The posts reached less than halfway to the ditchbank. He wanted to go back up the hillside the next day and cut more posts, until he had all he needed, but he knew he'd lost. He could go back to the fenceline after haying, but it wouldn't be the same. He had wanted to get through with it before haying, and he'd lost. Now there would be too much work on the fence after haying. The work would be hot and endless, and there wouldn't be time left for him and Blueboy to go to the mountains. He'd been fooling himself about the mountains all along. The old man would never have let him go anyway.

The sun was down, the air was cooling fast. Exhausted, Cloyd leaned on the last post. He felt chilled one minute, burning up the next. He feared he might have fever from the ticks in the oakbrush. When he looked down the line of fenceposts, it seemed senseless, what he'd done. The day before, he'd received a letter from his sister, and he didn't even know what it said. He could read a few words, but that was all. He was too embarrassed to ask the old man to read it to him. He longed for White Mesa. All he wanted was to go home. Looking across the field to the gray farmhouse in the trees, he wondered what had made him think he could belong here.

Walter was in the house, fixing a special supper for Cloyd. He'd been planning it all week: a Thanksgiving-style dinner with turkey and all the extras. He'd taken the day off to prepare the meal, but he hadn't been able to talk Cloyd out of working on the fenceline. When Cloyd finally came in, later than usual, he hadn't even a nod for the old man. Walter could see how gloomy he was. Cloyd shoved his plate away after picking at the turkey. Walter, who never ate much, began to put away the mountain of leftovers.

In the parlor, Walter sought out his recliner. Cloyd collapsed with a sigh on the sofa. Walter glanced at his new *Mining Gazette* but set it aside. Something was terribly wrong, and he'd have to get the boy to tell him what it was. What could he say? Maybe he should try a new tack. "Tell me about that letter you got yesterday," he suggested awkwardly. "What do you hear from home?"

Cloyd battled the confusion washing over him. He felt angry at the old man, and he didn't know why. He thought about the letter in his pocket. What should he say?

"It's my letter," he said finally. "It's none of your business."

Walter felt sorry he had chosen the letter to try to talk about. "I didn't mean to pry, Cloyd," he apologized.

"I don't know what's in the letter!" Cloyd shouted, standing up. "I can't read it. I don't know how. There, are you satisfied?"

He felt the weight of the old man's eyes on him.

Leaning forward, the old man reached out and touched Cloyd's hand. The dark veins stood out on his forehead. "I'm sorry, Cloyd," he whispered. "I had no idea. Let me read it for you. Where's the letter?"

Cloyd wanted to hear the letter, but he hated his weakness being suddenly out in the open. Now the old man would think that he was stupid.

"Why, I could maybe help you in the evenings," Walter was saying. "And I could sure read you these mining papers. . . ."

"I don't want your help," Cloyd said. He had to get away.

In his confusion he bumped into the table and spilled the old man's coffee all over the mining newspapers. He had to get to his room and be by himself.

"Leave me alone," he shouted at Walter as he ran for the stairs. "Leave me alone!"

8

In the morning Cloyd was surprised to find Walter acting as if nothing had happened. "Time to buck them bales out of the field and up into the barn," the old man said cheerfully. Cloyd didn't respond. How could things ever be the same between them again? He kept his eyes on his plate and said nothing.

After breakfast, three pickups pulling horsetrailers drove into the farm. Two of the trucks were loaded heavily with saddles and camping equipment. The third carried at least a dozen barking hound dogs. Six men in blaze-orange vests got out of the trucks as the old man waved and walked down the drive to meet them. Had the old man been expecting them? Cloyd wondered. He hadn't talked about anyone coming.

The leader, very tall and sure of himself, stood in front of the rest and made small talk with the old man. Cloyd watched from behind a tractor in the shop. The tall man took off his cowboy hat, revealing a headful of wavy red hair. The wind, blowing in Cloyd's direction, carried their words to him. The two talked easily about Walter's new beard and his peaches. Apparently they were good friends.

The others standing around began to fidget, Cloyd saw. They were strangers. One of them asked in a Texas accent, "Does the wind always blow like this in Colorado?"

Cloyd saw the tall, red-haired man turn his shoulder and wink to Walter. "A question like that you oughta ask Walter here. Heck, I was just a kid when he invented this whole country. What about this wind, Walter—think it'll let up?"

The old man tugged at his cap. "It's been known to blow, that's for certain. Just workin' up to it this morning. Myself, I like to keep track of the wind by hangin' a chain on a post. If it stands out straight, that's a breeze, but when it gets to whippin' around and links snap off, why look out—it's likely to get windy by sundown."

Walter told it straight-faced, but when he finished he held his breath, and his ears turned red. Everyone was laughing. The old man's cheeks were all puffed out. Finally he blew the air out his nose, his head bobbing, and he stroked the white whiskers on his chin. "Yes sir," he concluded, "It can blow—not that it does very often."

Cloyd was amazed at how easily the old man got

on with these people, laughing with them and having a good time. He hadn't even met some of them before. Who were these people?

Still laughing, the men turned to their preparations. Cloyd came out of the shed and watched them unload the horses. After they parked their trucks and trailers out of the way, they packed the horses, shouting instructions back and forth. Walter came over to Cloyd and said the tall man was his old friend. Walter was all excited, like the man was really important. "Rusty's the best outfitter in the San Juans," he said. "Best outdoorsman I ever saw. More'n likely he'll scare up a bear."

The red-haired man beckoned to Walter from beside the coal pile, where he was rigging the horses. The old man went to him and then into the house, returning with the salt and pepper shakers from the kitchen table. Suddenly Cloyd realized that these men had to have the old man's permission to hunt on his land, and that he had already given it to them. To hunt for bears?

With no warning, the old man was bringing the red-haired man over. "Got someone I'd like you to meet, Rusty," he said to his friend. "This here's Cloyd."

For an instant, before he looked away, Cloyd saw the bear hunter's eyes. The man thought that meeting Cloyd was a joke. The tall man stuck out his giant hand, and said in his raspy voice, "Glad to meet 'ya. 'Cloyd,' is it? Never heard a name like that before."

Walter had never tried to shake hands with Cloyd. Cloyd hated shaking hands. But he had no choice but to offer his now.

The red-haired man didn't just shake his hand, he crushed it. He didn't have to do that, Cloyd thought. It hurt really bad. Cloyd tried not to let his face show the pain. He glimpsed the man's mocking eyes. The eyes said Cloyd was nothing, nothing at all, only an Indian.

The old man was trying to get them to talk. "Cloyd here's real good with horses," Walter said, beaming. "That blue roan of mine has really taken a shine to him."

"Is that so?" the outfitter said with a short laugh. "Well, a horse ain't a dog, Cloyd. It could care less about you. All it cares about is getting fed. A horse is a work animal, not a pet."

Cloyd turned away. His hand was still throbbing. The bear hunter turned to his own business and mounted his horse. Cloyd imagined what he could do to the red-haired man's hand if he were twice the man's size. Break every bone in it.

Cloyd watched the riders and their dogs disappear upriver. He was furious, and the old man didn't even know it. Cloyd was sure now that he meant nothing to the old man. These men were his real friends. And they were bear hunters.

It was time to bring in the hay. The old man was going to drive the tractor, and he was supposed to buck the bales onto the trailer and afterward stack them up in the barn. The old man, he recalled, liked to brag about how heavy his bales were—eighty pounds. "People get their money's worth," he'd said. Eighty pounds was fine for Walter—the old man wasn't planning on bucking the bales himself. That would be Cloyd's job.

The old man was standing by the tractor, waiting, but Cloyd walked off down to the riverbank instead. A few minutes later he heard the tractor's motor fire. The old man was going to go ahead without him. Let him try, Cloyd thought. It's his hay, not mine.

Along the riverbank he saw several magpies and then a raven. They reminded him of the canyons back home, and his sister, and he grew powerfully homesick. He brought the bearstone out of his pocket and tried to make a wish on it that he could go home. But the stone only reminded him of where he was and what the red-haired man was going to do. In a sudden burst of awareness he felt like he was the bear the man was after, and he could feel what it would be like to be chased by barking dogs and men on horses. He knew with awful certainty that the bear would be run down, cornered, and killed. Maybe it would be the mother bear, the one he'd seen with the cub. It was the old man's fault, he decided bitterly—he'd given his permission. If they killed a bear, the old man would have to pay. The old man never cared about me, he thought, these are his real friends.

Walter decided to bring in the hay all by himself. Something was wrong with Cloyd, he knew, but he shouldn't have walked off on him when he was needed most. Well, he would show this boy what Walter Landis was made of. He'd bucked a few bales in his life. Jumping off and back on the tractor, he pitched bale after bale onto the trailer like he was a young man again. His face was flushed bright red, his breathing came louder and louder, but he wouldn't quit. He brought load after load to the barn, heaving and grunting and dragging the bales into place. He'd work until all the hay was in or his heart burst, whichever came first. He didn't care which.

He worked all morning and never came in for a meal. He worked all through the long afternoon, through the dusk, and into the darkness, until the last bale was up in the barn. Then he walked silently into the house, neglecting to take off his boots or his cap. Tracking dirt on the white parlor rug, he disappeared into his room, trailing bits of hay.

Walter was exhausted. He lay on his bed in his soiled overalls and boots and talked to his wife. "Maude," he said, "I'm an old fool, but I just don't know what to do with this boy. I sure wish you were here to help me. Something's got into him—I don't know what. He was doing so good. I guess we'll just hang on and see what happens. . . ."

The house fell silent. Cloyd was in his room, packing his duffel bag. The old man would get rid of him now. Tomorrow, he'd be back at Eaglewing. That would be all right. He didn't care anymore.

9

At first light, Walter was usually up and cooking sausage and eggs. Cloyd waited awhile for him in the kitchen, then took a loaf of bread and a jar of peanut butter outside. It was easy to put off seeing the old man.

Several hours later Walter limped out of the house. Cloyd was surprised to see he had shaved his beard off. "Hay's in the barn, Cloyd," he announced cheerfully. "Lucky it didn't get rained on. Once you're into July—and today's the first—you're pressin' your luck."

Cloyd didn't know what to say. The old man was acting like nothing had happened.

"Wouldn't mind a bit if it rained anytime now,"

Walter continued. "Wouldn't have to irrigate so much. I'd better start the water back in today—the field's drying out bad. How 'bout you? Got anything in mind? Maybe you'd like to take that roan—"

"Make some more posts, I guess," Cloyd mumbled.

Walter hesitated. "Fine," he said uncertainly. "That's just fine."

Cloyd trudged across the field with the saw and the gas can. He'd left behind the pint of oil Walter wanted mixed with the gas.

It was another cloudless day. The last of the night's lingering cool air was burning off as he angled through the haystubble toward the hillside.

Before he climbed, he took a good look at his fenceposts, marching stout and straight all the way to the peach orchard. It was a strange feeling; they looked different. They didn't make him feel proud or good. They weren't his anymore.

He'd forgotten to bring along any drinking water. Already he was thirsty, and the sun was blazing. His head was pounding. Why was he still here? He'd expected to be sent on his way back to Durango, and instead he was being sent back to work as if nothing had happened.

He had to get out of the sun. He veered away from the hillside and followed the posts down to the orchard. He dropped the saw, lay in the grass at the base of the big boulder, and looked up at the trees. He could lie there all day, he thought. Ever since he'd come to the old man, there'd never been time to look at the world this way that he liked.

Suddenly the bear was back in his thoughts, and

he could see it all happening. Men riding hard to keep up with their yapping dogs, the bear exhausted and desperate with no place to hide. He hated the outfitter, that red-haired man, with all his heart.

His thirst brought him back to the orchard. He swallowed hard and bitterly. The whole orchard was exploding with growth. The countless rock-hard peaches grew larger by the day—he'd been checking on them since the first day he came to the farm. He'd admired them, but now he hated them. These thriving trees of Walter's with their long, green leaves were so superior to his grandmother's it made him sick. Hers were pitiful.

He spat, but nothing came out. He had a bitter taste in his mouth, like poison. His grandmother's peaches were rare and beautiful only in the way he used to see them, not as they really were. But the old man's trees could have all the water they wanted, while his grandmother's, with their misshapen trunks and stunted, yellowed leaves, stood here and there against the sun and depended on the rain. Sometimes the rains didn't come at all and the peaches shriveled on the trees and there was no moisture to suck out of them.

All at once he heard dogs barking and men calling—the outfitter and his bear hunters had returned. Cloyd ran up the road toward the house, where the men had dismounted and were showing off their kill to Walter. Everyone talked at once, except for the red-haired man, who was acting like it was all in a day's work. A bear was heaped atop a nervous horse. It wasn't as big as Cloyd would have thought. It looked about like a big black dog. The old man was going to let his friend butcher it right there and hang it up in one of his sheds.

As if he were invisible, he walked among the preoccupied hunters with them taking no notice of him. He approached the bear and stared at it. The bear had nearly bitten its tongue in two. Its mouth was choked with clotted blood. A fly walked on one of its eyes.

Recounting the hunt, the men poked fun at each other. One man, the one who'd asked the old man about the wind, was especially happy—he was the one who shot it. "Bearskin for the den," he said proudly.

"Plenty of good sausage, too, and some for Walter here," the red-haired man said in his raspy voice. "What don't make sausage I'll feed to my dogs."

Suddenly Cloyd remembered all the sausage he'd eaten at the old man's table. It almost made him retch to think it might have been—probably was—*bear* meat he'd eaten all those mornings. He backed out of the clearing in front of the house, turned and ran back toward the peach orchard. A terrible revenge was taking shape in his mind.

Cloyd snatched up the saw from the tall grass at the base of the boulder. He filled it with gas, pink instead of its usual purple, the way it looked with the oil added in. Right now he didn't care how Walter wanted it. The old man was just fussy—he wouldn't even drive his truck without checking the oil first. Everything Walter did had to be in neat lines, like his windrows and his fences. Everything had to be so clean, like the white rug in his parlor and his tractors, and everything had to be in its place in the house, the sheds, and the barn.

He grabbed up the saw and yanked the pull-cord

with the saw in midair, as Walter had advised him never to do. The engine fired immediately and he gunned it until it screamed.

Cloyd wondered why he'd liked Walter in the first place, this fussy old white man who had a thousand times more than he needed and still had to have someone else do his work for him so he could get more. Maybe he'd worked for the old man because of finding the bearstone the first day. It was easy enough to see now—there was no connection between the good-luck token and the old man. Cloyd remembered how Walter laughed with the red-haired man and the other bear hunters when they first arrived. Laughs with Bear Hunters should be the old man's secret name, he thought bitterly.

He cut through the skin of the nearest tree and winced as he withdrew the saw. Beads of moisture were forming along the edges of the fresh wound. From one to the next he ran with the saw roaring at full throttle, and he cut each of the twenty-two peach trees most of the way through. Each time, as the saw's teeth bit into the thin bark, he hollered with hurt as if he felt the saw himself. He didn't want to cut them down, he wanted them to die slowly. Before they died, their leaves would yellow and the peaches shrivel, and they would look just like his grandmother's peaches.

Now he knew he was in big trouble, but that made it easier. He was only getting started. This time there wouldn't be any doubt he was going back to Eaglewing.

His mind racing and his throat so dry it seemed jammed with a wad of wool, Cloyd stumbled out of the orchard with the heavy saw. When his fifty-seven posts came into view all standing straight and lined up so perfectly, he pulled up for breath and caught himself admiring them. But what was the fence really for? To keep a man from crossing a field. It was a stupid reason to have worked so hard. At White Mesa he went with the goats wherever he wanted. None of the Utes put up fences or claimed a part of the mesa for their own. The animals went where there was feed, and there were no fences at all until some white men chained the trees out by their roots, dragged them into the arroyos, and fenced the northern end of the mesa for beans.

Cloyd tried his shoulder against the first post. It wouldn't budge. He had set them deep, wedging rocks around the posts and packing them with clay soil. They'd set up like concrete. Why should Walter be so concerned about some people hunting deer and elk on his ranch while he thought it was fine for others to hunt bears? He was a fool to have worked for the old man.

The juniper posts wouldn't rot in two hundred years, but he didn't want them there at all. The field looked better without them.

The saw didn't want to start. After dozens of attempts Cloyd made it idle erratically, but it cut out as soon as he tried the throttle. Eventually it caught at full throttle, and he discovered it would run if he didn't let up even a little bit. He walked along the line, sawing down the posts and thinking about people he didn't like. One post for the reading teacher who tried to make him read aloud, one for the speech teacher who always tried to make him get up in front of the class, and one for the nervous principal who was always saying, "Well, I guess I'll just have to use the board on you." One for each of the bear hunters. Two, three, four, five, six, sixteen for Walter and his friend, the red-haired man.

Half the posts remained when the saw began to kill as soon as it bit into the wood. Then it wouldn't fire at all. Cloyd checked the gas, which hissed as he loosened the cap. Boiling hot, most of it escaped. Maybe the saw did need oil mixed in with the gas, but who cared?

The saw was too hot; it wasn't going to start. Probably he'd ruined it by leaving out the oil. He felt like he was going to faint. He had to get out of the sun. He threw the saw down and walked off, waded the irrigation ditch at the edge of the field. Even though the water ran cool and clear, he didn't think to drink any. He started up the mountainside toward the sandstone outcrop where he'd found the blue stone.

On his way up, Cloyd saw the trucks and horse-trailers leave, and then he saw the old man walk down to the peach orchard. He turned and fled higher. When he reached the top of the cliffs and looked out, he was not soothed, as he had expected to be. The sight of the distant peaks did nothing to lift him out of the despair drowning him inside. Usually after he did something he knew was going to bring trouble, he felt better in a way—revenged. But with the old man it was different. He'd never felt this awful in his life; he'd never liked anybody this much, as much as he'd liked Walter. Suddenly he felt more alone than ever before, even more than in the first days in Durango after the tribe had sent him to Eaglewing.

This wasn't the same as getting into trouble with

the teachers or the principal, or with his housemother. Those people were making him do things he didn't want to do. It was different with the old man. Once, he had really wanted to work for Walter, and it was good then. Now everything was spoiled. He had spoiled it.

His thirst grew so bad he couldn't swallow. But he was good at enduring pain. No one could ever take that away from him. Maybe he would run away. But first he would stand up to the old man for punishment the way he did with the principal, then go home and hide in the canyons. Walter would take him back to Eaglewing, but he wouldn't stay for long. No one could find him in the canyons.

10

It was dark, and Cloyd was off the mountain. As he reached for the latch on the front door, the old man stepped out of the shadows, trembling with rage. He caught the boy by the shoulders with unnatural strength and shook him back and forth against the door. "What the hell's the matter with you, anyway?" he roared.

Cloyd said nothing and let himself be shaken. He'd spent his own anger and had none left to counter the enormity of the old man's wrath.

Walter put his livid face against Cloyd's where the boy's eyes couldn't avoid his. "Who the hell are you to come in here and ruin our peaches? You knew damn well what those trees meant to me. Well? Speak to me!"

Cloyd turned his head aside and looked at the ground.

"Give me that little blue rock you keep in your pocket," Walter commanded.

Cloyd's mouth turned sharply down at the corners. "What rock?" he grunted.

Walter extended his hand, palm up. "Give it to me, Cloyd. I wasn't born yesterday. I've seen you more'n once sneakin' it in and out of your hand. C'mon, give it!"

There was nothing else to be done. He could see he owed it to the old man. He heaved a sigh and fetched it out of his pocket.

Walter took the stone and closed his fist on it. "You care about this little rock, eh? You won't say? I think you do. C'mon, I want to teach you something."

Walter stalked over to his machine shop with the boy in tow, flicked on the bare bulb suspended from the rafters, and set the blue stone on his anvil. Then he reached for the sledgehammer.

"A dose of your own medicine," the old man raged, holding the sledgehammer high over his head.

Cloyd's heart turned to lead. He waited passively for his punishment.

As Walter focused on his target, he paused with the hammer in midair and craned his neck in the bad light. "What the hell is that thing?" he demanded.

"A bear," the boy answered quietly.

"A bear?" The old man took it in his hand and examined it up close. Cloyd edged forward.

"You care about this thing quite a bit, don't you?"

Cloyd wouldn't say. He backed off and looked at the ground.

59

"Oh, to hell with it," Walter stormed. "Here, keep it."

When Cloyd didn't respond, Walter reached over and shoved it into his pocket. "Go get your stuff. I just want to get the hell rid of you."

It was late at night. As the pickup wound slowly through the foothills on its way to Durango, each of them kept silent, preoccupied with his own regrets. Just after they passed through the little town of Bayfield, the headlights illuminated a rabbit darting across the highway. Walter and Cloyd both winced at the thump under the wheels. In their broodings, that thump resounded like a judgment, and each was plunged deeper in remorse.

Fifteen more slow and silent miles, and they reached Durango. Walter stopped at a red light and stared down Main at the blinking yellows. At this hour Durango was a ghost town, and it seemed there were only the two of them in the world. "I couldn't miss him," Walter said with a sigh.

"Miss who?" Cloyd asked quickly. Somehow he was eager to talk with the old man.

"Oh, that darned rabbit back there. He seemed bound and determined."

"It wasn't your fault."

"I suppose not," Walter said slowly. "Just one of them things. Well, show me the way to your . . . Eaglewing."

Cloyd gave directions, and then the old man geared the truck down, and it crept toward the group home. They both knew they had only a few minutes left. "I wonder if you'd mind if I looked over that turquoise piece of yours once more," Walter said.

The old man turned it over in his fingers, eyed it, and rubbed it thoughtfully, but he said nothing as he drove down the empty streets.

"Turn here," Cloyd said.

Walter sighed. "It's a sure-enough bear," he said. "Could even be a grizzly, from the shape of it. I went to the Bear Dance once down at the reservation. . . ." he began, then stopped talking. A revelation was forging itself in his mind. At last he said, "You cut those peaches right after those fellows came in from their bear hunt. Isn't that right?"

Cloyd grimaced.

Walter scratched and scratched behind his ear, and then he handed the stone back. "Well, that helps some, it sure does."

"Here it is," Cloyd said, and pointed to the house with his lips.

Walter slowed to a stop and eyed the group home. It wasn't what he expected; you couldn't tell it apart from all the other tract homes in the neighborhood. He drove on another block before he stopped. For a long time he said nothing. He took off his cap and raked his bald head with his fingers. Then he said, shaking his head a little, "Pigs might fly, but they're unlikely birds."

"What's that mean?"

"Just an old saying," he replied with a faint smile. "I never did know exactly, but I always liked the sound of it. Cloyd, Susan told me once you'd rather more'n anything just go home. Is that right?"

Cloyd shrugged guardedly.

"Well?"

"They won't let me."

"I suppose not," Walter agreed, as he slipped the truck into gear and drove off.

"What're you doing?" Cloyd mumbled.

"Takin' you home."

"How come?"

"You ain't gonna do any good here at this 'Eagle-wing,' are you?"

"They won't let you."

"I don't see nobody," Walter said gruffly.

"They'll come and get me."

"I'll wait a week before I tell Susan. You'll have some time at home, whatever happens."

They left Durango behind and headed west up a steep grade. Cloyd barely thought about going home, he was so astonished and puzzled. He didn't know what to make of this old man. He'd liked him, and then he'd hated him, and now he didn't know what to think. Walter was taking him home. After a few more miles had passed and they were on their way down the western side of the mountains, he asked again, "How come you're doing this?"

"Maybe it'll help you get the bee out of your bonnet," the old man said coldly.

Cloyd didn't want to have to ask him what that meant. The old man was in a strange mood—better to keep quiet. He thought about the horse. He wished there'd been a chance to see Blueboy before he left.

The sun was rising over the high desert as they neared White Mesa. In the clear, thin air Cloyd took in the landmarks he'd grown up with. He almost wished he could share them with Walter, but they hadn't really made a peace. To the north, Blue Mountain, the sacred one, still wearing a patch of snow. To the east, the massive form of the Sleeping Ute lying on his back with arms folded across his chest, not yet ready to awake and vanquish his enemies. To the south, the glowing white cliffs of the San Juan as it flowed through Bluff, and beyond them the bare redlands of the Navajos with the towers of Monument Valley beginning to appear in the early light. To the west, the wooded slope of Cedar Mesa falling from the Bear's Ears to the river, gouged by the bottomless red-walled canyons. In those remote canyons was where he would hide, he decided. There, in the slickrock country, he could live wild and free.

As they drove south out of Blanding onto the windy mesa, Cloyd searched for something to say to thank the old man. There was something welling up inside him that he'd never felt before and that had to be expressed. Too soon he was pointing out the nondescript government house that was his grandmother's, the one with the summer ramada of cottonwood branches on one side and the scraggly peach trees on the other. And then he was standing by the truck with his duffel bag in his hand, and the old man was saying, "Good luck, Cloyd. Let's don't say good-bye with no hard feelin's. . . ."

Cloyd nodded, but it was all happening too fast, his feelings were too deep to be reached. He found no words at all, only waved slightly as the old man turned the truck around and drove away.

The pickup was small in the distance by the time he realized he'd lost something of priceless value. He waved forlornly, then furiously, as the truck vanished. With the suddenness of a cloudburst in the desert, tears ran down his face.

He stumbled around behind the house to the little shed and corral, to check in on the goats. They were all gone. There was no fresh dung there, either.

After smoke started to come from the chimney pipe, he went in. His grandmother looked up from the frybread dough she was kneading and gave a sharp cry.

A Ute woman in the old style, she was dark, earthy, and large, the mainstay of her diet being frybread. In her green velveteen blouse and voluminous red skirt, and in the way she knotted her long hair and wrapped it in bright yarn, she reflected the influence of the nearby Navajos. Not one to ask a flurry of questions, she made a joke about his ribs showing through his T-shirt and opened up a can of fruit cocktail. It was something for him to start on while she cooked the frybread in the oil she had boiling on the cookstove. She fed the people in her life, lavished affection on them, rarely asked anything, and never tried to control whether they came or went.

They squeezed honey on their frybread. Cloyd wanted to talk. He'd spoken no Ute in the last year, as the boys from the Colorado reservation no longer knew the language. Right away he found himself telling her about Walter, how they'd worked together, how there was a river flowing right through his farm.

"Good," she said. "I knew you would like it in Colorado."

He told her about the high mountains, how someday he'd like to go there and climb the highest peak he could find.

"Wouldn't that be something," she said, her eyes

reflecting the vision. "This man you work for, he lives in a good way?"

"He's the best man I ever knew," Cloyd heard himself saying. "He's old—older than you. His wife died. He's all alone."

Suddenly he knew he had no desire to hide out in the canyons. But what was he to do?

They talked about his sister who was at the boarding school in Salt Lake City. She had visited, his grandmother said, and had reported that everything was fine.

"I'll go to Blanding on Saturday and get lots of groceries so we can put some fat on your ribs."

Though sometimes someone she knew stopped and picked her up, often enough she walked all the way. Cloyd saw how he could save her the ten miles into Blanding, ten miles back. He realized he'd made a decision. "Oh, I can't stay long," he said. "I have to leave tomorrow."

His grandmother's eyebrows rose. "Oh?"

"Walter needs me. We have a lot of work to do."

"Well, that's good. I'm glad you came to see me. How are you traveling?"

Cloyd gave the hitchhiking sign with his thumb.

"I have to go now," she said. "I have a job. There is a day-care center here now. I cook for them. I had to sell the goats when there was nobody to take care of them. Maybe someday we'll get them back." She paused at the door. "Live in a good way," she said in parting, as she always did.

Cloyd decided to leave right away. His grandmother would understand. But would the old man take him back?

11

When Walter got home from Utah, he went directly to his bed and collapsed in his dirty overalls. He was exhausted. Unshaven, no sleep, nothing to eat, at his age driving to Utah and back: he'd been letting himself go to the dogs. And he didn't care. Right now he should be irrigating the field. The grass would burn up in the heat before long if he didn't. But he didn't care. He let himself sink into sleep like a heavy stone plunging into a well.

When he woke up he was hungry. Intent on drowning himself in sentiment, he went downstairs to the basement to fetch a jar of peaches. He sat on a crate a long time as the sunken window admitted less and less light. He brooded on the two dozen or so jars of peaches left on the shelf, her special Missouri peaches from those seedlings she'd brought along to Colorado. He'd told her that peaches wouldn't make it here, but she insisted. And there'd never been a time he'd gone downstairs for peaches that he hadn't remembered how it all happened.

Walter studied the crack that had appeared the length of the concrete basement wall just after his wife died. He got up and looked at it from across the room and then from the corner, where he eyeballed the length of the wall. He saw, or feared he saw, the foundation bulging in more than ever. As he had many times before, he outlined the work that had to be done to plumb the wall. Digging, pouring, timbering . . . He had the materials, the tools, the know-how—everything but the desire.

He didn't care anymore. About much of anything. He had for a while, when the boy was with him and they were working together to put the farm back in order. To what purpose? he wondered. He'd tried to make it like it was before, when his wife was alive, when the two of them and the farm were all one. On the surface, he and Cloyd had succeeded. But a farm isn't land and fenceposts and hay in the barn. As his wife always said, "A farm is a home." He'd failed the boy. When he'd had the chance to give him a home, he'd given him only work. But work for work's sake can't keep a soul going, Walter told himself. That's like pounding rocks in a prison yard. It's not the work that's awful, it's the lack of purpose.

She was gone. He could quit working the farm now. He himself had never been a farmer. He was a miner. He'd taken up farming for her, and gladly. They'd had all those good years making their living on the farm.

67

Now he could quit, and lie down to rest. . . .

The next morning, Walter got up late and wandered outside to check on the horses. They had plenty of pasture and were able to drink from the river, but there was no telling when one might turn a leg in a varmint hole or get itself torn up in barbed wire. He felt bad when he saw the blue roan. He was never going to look at that horse again without thinking of the boy.

On the way back, he walked the irrigation ditch to see if a beaver hadn't moved in and started to dam it up. He sat down on the ditchbank with all the hay-fields sloping away in front of him and tried to think of how to get his fields taken care of properly. Only one choice remained, really; he'd just been putting it off. He'd pick the best man he could and lease the second cutting to him. There were always industrious fellows around trying to raise more cows than they had the land to support. They had families to feed and mortgages to pay off. He'd turned down plenty of requests as they'd seen him getting older.

He didn't really have to work anymore. The farm had been paid for years ago, and he didn't need much income to live the way he did. They'd always put some savings by, and he got a steady, if small, income from the mining claim his wife had finally convinced him to sell, the one near Monarch Pass. She'd wanted him to sell the Pride of the West, too, but he was so adamant about keeping it, she finally gave up. She even quit badgering him about his packhorses and mining equipment, and his occasional announcements that in a year or two he might reopen his mine. So many years had gone by, she knew he was just hanging on to a dream he'd had when he was young, and there wasn't any harm to it.

It was pleasant to sit on the ditchbank in the morning sun and imagine he was up at the mine, sitting on the ore dump with Snowslide Creek rushing by and the peaks all around, the grass green and the wildflowers all in bloom. And inside the mine, not far at all from where he'd left off tunneling, waited the heart of the mountain, a secret place, a marvelous fluke made millions of years before in the bowels of the earth: a room having no doors, its furniture and draperies the fantastic shapes of glistening, crystalline gold.

Walter looked up to see a figure stumbling toward him out of the dying peach trees and through the sawed-off fenceposts lying at sixes and sevens down at the low end of the farm. The figure was struggling with an awkward burden. The old man squinted for a better look. In a few moments, to his everlasting amazement, he made out the white T-shirt and jeans, the duffel bag, the shaggy black hair and the brown face of the boy. He stood up meekly, lifted his cap, and ran his trembling hand over and over his skull. "He's come back, Maude," he said quietly. "He's come back." Then he walked down to meet the boy.

They stood face-to-face in the middle of the field.

"I want to try again," Cloyd said, looking away.

Walter shook his head in wonder.

"Please, I'll do better," the boy pleaded, thinking he'd been turned down.

"My goodness, Cloyd, of course you can. Maybe I can do better, too."

The boy pointed toward the orchard with his lips. "I'm sorry about the trees."

"I see you are. Both of us was hurt bad. I like to think, though, that the hurt you get over makes you stronger. Now let's get you taken care of. You look like something the cat spit out."

Cloyd smiled wearily, and they walked down to the house. He showered, ate some sandwiches, and went upstairs to bed. When he woke up, Walter had his clothes cleaned and dried for him. Cloyd asked what work he should do next. Walter explained that he was leasing out the farm and wouldn't be working it anymore. "I've been thinking up a storm today, Cloyd. I don't have that much time left in my life—I'm old enough, I oughta be able to do what I really want. Farmin' was good to me, but now it's time to quit. I ain't a mule turnin' grist. What I'm tryin' to say is, do you remember how I've got a mine up in the back country?"

"The Pride of the West?"

"That's right. Remember how I said I'm gonna re-open it someday? I've been sayin' that for years. Well . . . now, I figure, now's the time. I'd need your help gettin' up there, of course, but if I remember right, you were always askin' about the mountains. I think it might do us both a world of good to get up into that high country. How would that suit you, Cloyd?"

"Will we take the horses?"

"Of course. No roads in there. We'll have to pack in everything."

Cloyd beamed. "Can I ride Blueboy?"

"You bet. I'll ride that sorrel mare."

70

"When can we go?"

"It might take a couple-three weeks to lease out the farm, get everything ready, and tie up all the loose ends. Tomorrow's the Fourth of July, so that still leaves us a good while up there before you have to be back in school. But before we get too serious about anything, let's take a day off. They got a rodeo up in Pagosa on the Fourth every year. I'm thinkin' you'd really enjoy it. You're about due for a payday—maybe you could spend some of your earnin's. And I'd get a chance to take those hot mineral baths they got there. Always does wonders for my bones."

Cloyd spent the afternoon riding Blueboy up the river and telling him the news about the mountains, over and over and over.

12

Today was the big day. Cloyd and Walter had been up since four in the morning shuttling the packhorses, mining equipment, food, and camping gear to the trailhead at the end of the road up the Pine River. It was midafternoon, and thunderclouds were gathering over the mountains. On their third and last trip to the trailhead, they stopped in Bayfield to buy a few last-minute supplies. Walter bought a fishing rod for Cloyd, and hooks and salmon eggs. "Used to be good fishing on the Pine—bet it still is. If the trout don't like the salmon eggs, you can dig worms with the camp shovel or catch grasshoppers. Maybe you can catch us some fresh dinner now and again."

They drove up the river road. Cloyd could hardly

believe he was finally going to the mountains. A few miles north, Walter pulled off by the Pine River Cemetery. He told Cloyd he could wait a few minutes or come along. Cloyd looked in on the saddle horses in the gooseneck trailer, Blueboy, and the old man's sorrel mare, while Walter walked into the little cemetery. Then he caught up with the old man in front of a pair of graves.

At the far end of the plot was centered a single stone. Cloyd recognized the name *Landis*. Underneath there were two names, and one of them was Walter's.

"Why is your name on this?" Cloyd asked in undisguised confusion.

Walter scratched the thick white bristles of his beard. It was almost grown out again. "All they have to do is put the date on. Makes it easy."

Cloyd picked dandelions and piled the flowers on the grass. He thought about Walter in a box under the grass. "Do you have any relatives?"

"There's a few still around. My brother's on the Animas River down in New Mexico, and my wife's kin are back in Missouri."

Suddenly the wind began to blow. Cloyd looked up from the gravestones and saw the black clouds racing toward them from the mountains, where lightning flashed and rain hung in dark layers. He was chilled in his T-shirt, but he wanted to hear Walter talk. "Are people still alive after they die—like they say?"

"I don't know, really. Lots of folks believe there's life after death, but nobody knows for sure. Maybe your life is all there is. But that's plenty, ain't it?

Make it good while you have it, is what I think, in case there ain't nothin' extra."

"Live in a good way. That's what my grandmother says."

"That's a fine way to put it."

The clouds overtook them and darkened the Pine River Valley. Thunder rumbled more frequently. A long bolt of lightning struck a few miles upriver, the concussion and unraveling thunder following behind. "Comin' our direction," Walter remarked with some anxiety.

Cloyd didn't want to cut off this talk with the old man. It was important. They could always run for the truck. "How come you stopped here—to talk to your wife?"

"Well, in a way. To tell her I'm goin' back to the mine, I guess."

"But she can't hear you."

"Prob'ly not, but it's more a matter of respect."

"How do you mean?"

"Showin' honor for her. I wouldn't do something this important without consulting her if she was alive. Matter of fact," he chuckled, "I wouldn't be doing it at all. But seeing the circumstances, she won't mind. She'd say, 'You go up there with Cloyd to that mine of yours and find your gold.'"

"But she isn't alive."

"No, that ain't right. Somehow, as long as I'm alive, she is too."

"Like she's a part of you?"

"People get like that, Cloyd. That's what's special about people."

The wind stopped abruptly, and Walter had that claustrophobic feeling he got when the air pressure was dropping fast around him. "Say, we better shake a leg," he said, and turned from the grave.

The old man wasn't much for running, but he shuffled along as briskly as he could. They were barely inside the truck when the wind and the rain struck. "Let's wait her out," Walter said. "No sense driving in this."

Cloyd reached into his jeans pocket and pulled out the bearstone, set it on the dashboard. "I want to tell you a secret about this," he said.

Walter appraised the stone up close, the turquoise bear he'd nearly destroyed in anger. "It's some piece," he said. "Forehead's dished out like a grizzly's, and this bulge here on the back, it's almost like it's a hump."

"I found it with one of the Ancient Ones—a baby—in those rocks up there, above your farm."

"In the cliffs? A burial? Why, if that ain't somethin'."

"Bears are special for Ute people—they bring strength and good luck."

"All the more reason you've got yourself something special here," Walter said. "Think how old this stone must be. This blue bear's a real treasure, Cloyd."

"When I found this, I gave myself a secret name. The Utes used to do that—they kept it secret except for one other person. You're the only one I'll ever tell my secret name to. It's Lone Bear. That's what it is—Lone Bear."

Walter conjectured what it might mean, the name

Cloyd had taken for himself. It seemed like an awfully lonesome name. He wondered if the turquoise piece would bring the good luck the boy was hoping for.

"You know, Cloyd, some of that good luck just might rub off on the Pride of the West."

13

Walter roused Cloyd when it was still dark in their camp at the trailhead. By the light of the gas lantern they set to work sorting their gear into eight loads for the eight packhorses. After sunrise Cloyd brought the horses into camp from the meadow by the river where they'd been hobbled overnight.

The packhorses stamped their feet and shied from the wooden frames lifted toward them. The packing dragged on all morning. Cloyd could hardly believe all the gear they were taking with them. Two groups of backpackers left up the trail while they were working. Finally the last knot was tied, the riding horses saddled. Cloyd and Walter led their animals to the wooden gate between the parking lot and the beginning of the trail.

"What's this sign say?" Cloyd asked.

"Weminuche Wilderness Area. No motorized vehicles beyond this point."

Cloyd looked up the trail and saw it climb through a dense stand of pines. The trunks weren't far enough apart to allow even a jeep through. "Why do they have to say that?" he asked.

"Why, that means motorbikes, I suppose, and snowmobiles in the winter. Good thing, too. Our horses are spooky enough without having to contend with motors. That 'Weminuche' there, that's the name of the Utes who used to live up here."

"I know. My grandmother said that's us. We're the Weminuche."

"Well, now ain't that somethin'."

And then they were under way, each leading a string of four packhorses. Walter rode in front on his sorrel mare; Cloyd followed on the big blue roan.

The canyon soon narrowed, and the trail climbed well above the river. Cloyd found himself looking down hundreds of feet into pools so clear he could see the stones on the bottom. Above them, rockslide paths fell through the spruce and aspen forests from the peaks. As high as they were, these peaks weren't the towering, jagged ones he'd seen from the cliffs that first day at the farm. Before long, he would stand on top of one of the very highest and look out over the world.

The farther they worked their way up the Pine, the more Cloyd marveled at the steady gait and sure-footedness of the roan. And when the horse had a chance, he'd swivel his eye back around and catch sight of the boy. There was something Cloyd had been turning over and over in his mind and now, he decided, was the time to ask the old man about it. "Is it true, like he said, that horses don't care anything about you?"

The old man hitched himself up in the saddle and halfway turned around. "You mean like Rusty said? Don't pay no mind to his talk. He just hates to agree with anybody. It's just the way he is."

"But is it true?"

"I've always puzzled on that, same as you. Horses appreciate good treatment and a steady hand, but it's a fact they don't go out of their way to fetch your slippers. Maybe some really do care. I've had one or two that made me think so, but it seems like you never know for sure. What do you think?"

"Oh, I was just wondering."

Cloyd was mostly disappointed with the old man's answer. As they rode, he continued to turn it over in his mind. He leaned forward and patted the roan. "Blueboy," he thought, "you're not just any horse. You and me, Blue, you and me."

The roan rolled an eye back and snorted loudly.

The next day the horses labored up ever-steeper grades as the river fell in leaps from the high country. Cloyd watched his string carefully as they crossed the tricky scree slides of fine rock that ran below them all the way to the river. Several times during the day they forded swift creeks that fed the Pine; with little urging, the roan crossed them easily. The others behind accepted his leadership.

Late in the afternoon they climbed out the canyon onto a large meadow, astonishingly green with knee-high grass and ringed by mountains that stabbed far above the line where the trees stopped growing. A small stream here close to the Continental Divide, the Pine River wound quietly in delicate meanders through the meadow. Walter said they'd lay over a day or two before they went up Snowslide Canyon to the mine. Cloyd was happy to make camp. As he'd been riding, he'd seen the trout darting through the riffles between the pools. They set up the sheepherder tent in the trees at the meadow's edge.

At first light Cloyd was up digging worms in the black soil underneath the trees. On the meadow, he sneaked up on a pool and let his bait drift into a likely spot. In a moment the rod came alive in his hands, and he launched the flashing trout into the air and over his head. A large cutthroat trout in its orange-red colors lay gasping in the grass. It was the first fish he'd ever caught and the beginnings of a meal for him and the old man. He remembered his grand-mother saying that when the Weminuche lived in the mountains, some of the men were so skilled that they could catch fish with their bare hands. That didn't seem possible. But now he knew how they must have felt when they caught the lightning-fast trout, how-ever they did it.

Midway up the meadow Cloyd caught his second trout, and then his third at the upper end where the stream came rushing out of the trees. He'd discovered the fishing was better if he kept trying new water than if he stayed with one hole, even if he could see plenty of trout there. It seemed they would strike pretty quick, or not at all. He decided to look upstream in the trees for another good place to fish. After walking around the rapids through a thick spruce forest, he found an even bigger, more promising meadow above.

As Cloyd began to fish the upper meadow, white clouds boiled up out of the blue sky and quickly turned dark. The wind started to blow, but he was too excited to notice the wind or the clouds—he was landing trout. Several miles from camp, at the far end of the upper meadow, he caught his seventh. As he slid the new-caught fish onto the stringer he'd fashioned from a willow branch, he shook with cold and realized the temperature had been dropping for some time. He'd been out fishing longer then he thought. Without the sun it was hard to judge the time, but it could be past noon already. He saw the clouds spill down the mountainsides toward him, dark and loaded with moisture. A few more pools, maybe one more fish, and he would collect his trout and head for camp.

Lightning broke loose and thunder rumbled, not too far off. A cold wind rushed down the meadow. He wished he'd worn more than a T-shirt, but he hadn't thought he would be out long. He knew he'd better run for it; the storm was about to break. As he picked up his stringer and started out, lightning cracked barely upstream. The shock wave and his surprise threw him to the ground. Glancing back, he saw the big spruces bending under the weight of the wind, and hail angling down with terrific speed.

Cloyd thought he could race the hail into the trees between the meadows and nestle in under a good roof of branches. He ran for the trees with the rod held high in his right hand and the stringer of trout in his left. He ran with a laughing heart because the hail was already pounding the meadow behind him, and yet at full speed he would outrun it just in time.

With no warning his right leg sank to the hip, his chest and face struck the ground, the rod and stringer of fish flew. In the tall grass, he'd failed to see the narrow trench connecting the stream with the pond where beavers had built one of their domed lodges.

Pain coursed through and through his leg. He was sure he'd hurt it badly. With his weight on his left knee, Cloyd dragged the right leg out of the beaver run and lay on his left side, watching the wall of hail advance down the meadow. He had to wait for the pain to clear. Lightning ripped the meadow simultaneously with its deafening thunder. A heartbeat later the hail struck, stinging him and bouncing all around in the grass. Within seconds he was drenched and started to shake with cold. His T-shirt and jeans clung to him; they offered no protection. The feeling went out of his fingers. He lay motionless, unable to think.

In minutes the meadow was carpeted with a layer of hail. All of a sudden, it was winter. Cloyd had seen hailstorms in the high desert, but not like this one. Here the air itself had turned freezing cold. Shaking now from fear as well as cold, he forced himself to think. Managing another hundred yards to the trees meant nothing now. He had to reach camp, the old man, and a fire—or freeze to death. He tried the leg. It could take some of his weight. Nothing was broken.

Cloyd knew he had to start out immediately, but somehow it seemed important not to leave the rod and the fish behind. They couldn't be far. As he raked through the hail-flattened grass with his sneakers, he realized he couldn't feel his feet. There was the rod. He scooped it up and clamped his fingers around it. Lucky for him it wasn't broken. And here were the trout, stiff and staring.

Then he ran as best he could, shaking, tripping, falling. The hail turned to cold and steady rain. Something told him that he had no chance in the woods, the way he came up from the lower meadow. He had to find a trail. Was there a trail? He hadn't seen one all day. Maybe there would be one on the far side of the meadow, across the stream.

Cloyd couldn't feel the icy water as he plunged across the Pine River holding up his rod and reel and his fish. In fact, he'd stopped shaking and couldn't feel anything at all. His body was getting too cold, much too cold.

Across the meadow he found a trail and hastened wildly down it. After a while he was in the trees. The trail fell sharply, muddy and slick, turning this way and that. He veered through dark shapes as if in a dream. No sign of the lower meadow and the old man, and the cold was squeezing the life out of him. Through the dark trees, off the trail and down by the stream, a small patch of orange caught his eye. His mind dismissed the image, but as he stumbled forward, the idea of the orange color slowly worked its way to the surface. It was a tent. Cloyd stopped and stared through the trees at a trace of blue smoke hanging in the dark branches above the tent.

He could barely move. It took him a long time to reach the orange tent. Now he stood dumbly by the remains of a fire. There was no fire here, only a bit of blue smoke curling around the soggy stub of a log.

Cloyd faced the tent. "I need help," he said thickly.

Someone lifted the tent flap—a young man with glasses and a dark beard—and cursed in surprise. The man came out of the tent, took away the rod and the fish, and forced him to the ground and inside the small orange tent. Cursing softly, the man said not to worry. He rummaged through a sack, muttering something about long johns.

The man with the beard pulled Cloyd's wet clothes off. The boy looked curiously at his own body. It didn't seem to belong to him. He noticed he wasn't shaking anymore. He didn't even feel cold. Then the man was dressing him in different clothes. It took a long time. His elbows kept poking the tent. Everything was orange, orange all around.

The bearded man stuffed Cloyd into a sleeping bag and asked if he felt warmer. He couldn't even answer. Then he was alone. The man had left. The cold and the quiet crept into one another comfortably. The world went dark; he felt himself falling asleep. He drifted deeper and deeper into the dark, like a leaf settling into the bottom of a deep pool. It was almost perfectly peaceful. He was so close to that perfect sleep when something intruded, one faraway nagging detail. He couldn't even tell what it was. After a while it was some kind of noise, very far away. A magpie or a raven squawking, or possibly even his sister come looking for him in the canyons and calling again and again. Yes, it was a human voice after all, nagging, calling, insisting, shouting, but it wasn't his sister. Gradually, light seeped into his eyes, and he saw a man with glasses and a black beard. Who was he?

BEARSTONE

The world was moving. No, he was moving, being dragged outside the orange tent into the dark trees, sleeping bag and all.

The man's glasses were fogged up. The man lay alongside him on his elbows blowing on the wet wood, making smoke. Some coals were glowing. The man kept wheezing on them. Finally they burst into a flame and the man placed a little stick across the flame and left again.

Branches were breaking somewhere. The tiny flame was gone. The man was back with his arms full of wood, and then he was on his elbows again, blowing until his face turned purple. The flame came back. The wood started to catch. The man left; branches were breaking. After a time he was back piling branches over the fire and blowing it into stronger and stronger flames. The flames grew brighter, bigger, stronger than the rain dripping from the trees.

The bearded man with fogged-up glasses was pulling him from the sleeping bag, standing him up close to the fire, arms locked around his chest. He could begin to feel the fire spreading warmth into his body. "You're going to be all right," the man was saying. Cloyd struggled to get free of the sleeping bag. The man unzipped it, let it fall, and gained a new hold on him. Cloyd struggled again. "Hang on there," the man cautioned, "you're still medium rare. I'm gonna cook you until you're charbroiled."

Finally Cloyd's eyes cleared, and the man turned him loose. He could stand by the fire on his own. The man went for more wood. After many trips he'd built a bonfire. At its edge he boiled water in an aluminum

85

pan and made coffee. When Cloyd drank it, he warmed from the inside out and at last became as warm as he could want to be.

"Think I'll clean your fish, if you don't mind," the man said. "They'd make a great hot meal for you, better than my freeze-dried stuff. You just stay by the fire there and make some more coffee if you like."

Cloyd nodded. The man went away through the trees to clean the fish at the stream. After he'd been gone some time, Walter rode into camp in his yellow rainslicker, leading the roan.

"Thank goodness you're okay, Cloyd," he said softly.

Walter's eyes took in the oversized clothes that weren't the boy's, a bruise below the right eye, a long scratch on his neck, the jeans and T-shirt drying by the fire. "I've been everywhere. I was afraid I wouldn't find you."

"I caught seven fish," Cloyd said.

The stranger came back with the fish cleaned and neatly arranged on the willow-branch stringer. Walter drank coffee with him and pieced together what had happened. Cloyd tended the frying trout.

The young man gave Cloyd a poke. "You must crave the taste of trout, the way you hung onto 'em."

A shy smile brightened the boy's face. "I guess so," he said.

Nothing ever tasted so warm or so good, Cloyd thought, as the three of them shared the fish. Except maybe new-made frybread.

Cloyd saw the worry finally leaving the old man's face. It seemed like the time to explain how he could have been so stupid. "I could have found a dry place in the trees, but I was running and fell into a hole."

The old man winked at the stranger and chuckled. "From the looks of it, the ground flew up and hit you in the face."

They all laughed. Cloyd pulled on his T-shirt and jeans. Not only dry, they were almost too hot for comfort. Walter went to his mare and pulled Cloyd's denim jacket from his saddlebags. Cloyd dismantled the fishing rod, then stood by the fire, turning his hands over even though they were warm already. He wanted to say something to the young man. He wouldn't have a chance to show it like with Walter. "Thank you," he said. Their eyes met for a moment. "You didn't have to . . . you didn't even know me, and you—"

"No big deal," the stranger said quickly. "You'd have done the same for me."

14

For two days they rested in their campsite by the meadow. When Cloyd recovered his strength, they set out for the mine. Past the upper meadow where Cloyd had been caught by the cloudburst, Walter reined in his mare and motioned the boy and his string of pack-horses alongside. "That canyon there," he pointed, indicating a steep-sided cleft in the mountains across the river, "that's Snowslide. The Pride of the West is on up it a ways. Won't be long now."

They forded the river and angled away from it up Snowslide Creek. Cloyd took a last look up the Pine River and knew at once he'd found what he'd been looking for. A single peak rising alone and high above the others had just come into view, a sharp peak riding alone in the turquoise sky. "What's that?" he called to the old man. "That mountain over there."

"That one yonder? Why, that's the Rio Grande Pyramid. Looks like one, don't it? That's where the Rio Grande River gets started—flows off the other side. That's quite a mountain, all right. Supposed to have been a grizzly and two cubs sighted on it about ten years ago."

"Grizzly bears?"

"That's right. Used to be plenty in this country, but that was some years ago. Of course we still have black bears."

"But this man saw three grizzly bears?"

"Says they was huntin' marmots just above the tree line. Most folks think he saw a big cinnamon, which is a black bear when he's brown. The last grizzly bear proven in the state of Colorado—or south of Wyoming, for that matter—was killed near here in 1954. It's on display in a museum up in Denver."

Cloyd fingered the smooth bearstone in his pocket. He wondered if it might really represent a grizzly, as Walter had suggested. He remembered that the old Utes especially honored grizzlies. "Do *you* think there's any more grizzly bears?" he asked.

"Don't know—most likely not. It's been a bunch of years since that fellow saw 'em, if that's what they were. But if he was right, and nobody's killed 'em since, the cubs'd be in their prime now."

"Do you think somebody probably killed them?"

"Not that anybody's heard about. But if a fellow was to kill one, he might not let on since they're protected now."

"What's that mean, 'protected'?"

"On account of being endangered. That means

there's so few of 'em that if anybody kills one, there might be none left, so it's against the law."

For several hours they rode up Snowslide Canyon, crossing many of the wide, grassy paths among the sun-whitened hulks of spruces ripped from the edges of the slides high above. At the bottom of one of the avalanche chutes, the old man and the boy found a big log and set out biscuits and canned pork for their midday meal. Walter pointed out the knee-high trees dotting the grassy route of the slide. "When they get just a bit bigger, the slide'll knock 'em down. They never quit trying, though. It's like building your house on a railroad track."

Scanning the skyline, the old man looked upstream. A smile crossed his face as he pointed up the canyon. "That peak with the ledge around the top like a crown sits directly above the mine. My tunnel's aimin' for the contact in the solid-gold heart of the mountain. The Pride of the West."

Cloyd thought about a heart made out of solid gold. It sounded like an awful cold heart. He didn't say so. "What's the contact?" he asked.

"A fissure vein of ore is what it is. Ore's the rock the gold is in. You see, gold is usually mixed with other minerals in veins that run through the mountain. If you find a good fissure vein, it'll never give out on you like a fault will. A fault leaves little pockets of ore called stringers. You find one of 'em, dig it out, and that's the end of it. But with a good fissure vein, you always have something to follow. Sometimes it'll narrow on you, maybe to inches, but then it'll widen out to eight feet or more."

Cloyd realized he would actually be mining soon,

inside a mountain in the dark. Up to now he'd thought about it hardly at all. At White Mesa most people thought of mining as a bad thing, though many of the men worked off and on in the mines or at the ore-shipping depot. The uranium made you get sick and die early, his grandmother said. She never said if gold made you sick. But then he remembered what she had said about gold. It made people crazy and dishonest. First the white men promised the Utes they could keep the mountains forever, but that was before gold was discovered and the miners came pouring in. The white men forgot all about their promise. The Utes were told to stay out of the mountains. They couldn't roam around anymore and live in the old way. They were given tiny reservations in the low country and told to stay there and grow corn.

"You really think there's gold in your mine?" he asked skeptically.

"Why, I know there is! I crossed a vein of silver already, but I didn't even bother to follow it, 'cause in those days silver wasn't worth much unless it was real high-grade ore. I got a three-hundred-foot tunnel in already, an' I figure from the geology there can't be more'n a few more to the contact. I ain't really gambling, Cloyd. Why, I already found the contact, you see, where the vein breaks the surface way up the mountain. It's tilted at a pretty good angle, and the idea of the tunnel is to reach it inside the mountain and then stope up to the surface."

"How come you didn't dig where you found it?"

"Sure wish I could have. But it's better mining sense to work upwards and let gravity move your rock for you—down ore chutes. It's too hard to move any quantity of rock uphill unless you've got heavy machinery."

The dubious cast to Cloyd's face told Walter he'd given the boy no feel for the joy of working in hard rock, the thrill of blasting and then returning to the drift always expecting to see a vein of high-grade ore laid open. "There's fabulous wealth in these mountains, Cloyd," he whispered reverentially. "And most of it hasn't been discovered yet. Let me tell you about the Cresson Mine up in the Cripple Creek District right here in Colorado. They were blastin' the face of the tunnel, following a fissure vein, and broke into a natural room forty feet long by twenty feet wide and fifteen feet high. A vug is what it was, like a geode— ever see a rock that's hollow in the middle with crystals all around? Well, this big room they found was a giant geode with the crystals sticking out the floor, the walls, the ceiling—everything was solid gold!"

It seemed from Walter's eyes that he was even now peering into the gold cave he'd described. Cloyd could see how much it meant to the old man. He would do his best for Walter, even though it sounded dark and cold and dangerous, and then he would climb the Rio Grande Pyramid for himself. "How much gold did they get from in there?" he asked politely, as the old man came out of his reverie.

"I recollect it was two and one-half million. At today's price—four hundred fifty dollars an ounce— that's be . . . thirty-some million dollars from that one room!"

They continued up the canyon until Walter stopped at a bend in the trail and stared across the creek where a great pile of tailings jutted from the mountainside.

"The Pride of the West," Walter whispered. "It took me nearly forty years to get back, but I finally made it. And my goodness, it doesn't look a bit different. Mountains don't get old very fast, Cloyd. This mountain, it's like it blinked while I went off a young man, looks again and sees me ridin' back plumb aged."

Walter and Cloyd set up the big sheepherder tent by the stream under a tall cluster of spruce. Once they had unpacked all the horses, they hobbled them in the grass across the creek where only a few rotted logs remained of the old man's corral. Then they climbed up the side of the ore dump and gained the landing on top, only to discover raw earth where the mine entrance should have been.

"Well, she's caved in, and not so long ago," Walter said, disappointed yet calm. "Just the portal, Cloyd. The topsoil slipped, is all. Inside it'll be fine, once we move this dirt out of the way. It's all hard rock once you're inside—we'll be in there drillin' in a few days."

"Drilling?" Cloyd asked vacantly. For a moment he'd hoped Walter would give it all up.

"Makin' holes in the rock—pretty deep—so we can slip the dynamite in and blast. We're going to have to do our drillin' the old way, with one of us holding the bit and the other pounding the sledgehammer. Slow going, but it works. They quit drilling by hand in the 1870s, way before my time. After that, double-jackin'—that's two men working like I said—was only for drilling contests or for fellows like me that didn't know any better mining back in the hills where you couldn't use machine drills. Drillin's hard work—can be dangerous, too."

"Dangerous?"

"One story I remember, there was these two men working high up on a scaffold in a big room inside a mine, and they were double-jackin' into the face up there. Must've been twenty-five feet up they was standing. Of a sudden their scaffolding busts, and the one doing the sledgework, he crashes down with it. Now his partner turning the bit, he grabs hold of his steel as he's falling, and it's stuck good and stout in the hole, so there he is hanging from it pretty as you please. He starts hollerin' for help of course, only his buddy's got nothing to help him with, and there's nobody else around. So after about five minutes, the fellow up above can't hold on no longer, and he crashes down, too. His buddy says, 'Dang—I knew you was slow, but I had no idea it'd take you five minutes to fall twenty-five feet!'"

"Is that a true story?"

"Yes sir, that's a true story," the old man said as he stroked the bristles on his chin. But quickly his ears turned red and his cheeks puffed in and out as he tried to hold his breath and keep from laughing.

"True?" Cloyd repeated gravely.

Walter's cheeks collapsed and his breath exploded. "True . . . and then some," he said, slapping his knees.

Cloyd had to laugh, too. It was good to be laughing with the old man.

15

It took three days of tedious handwork for them to clear the entrance. At last Cloyd's shovel broke through into empty space. He knelt and looked through the small opening. He saw only blackness but felt a steady flow of cool air escaping the mine through the hole he'd made. "Where's the air coming from?" he asked Walter.

"Oh, that's one of the lucky things about this mine—fresh air's always moving through it. Comes down from the surface through cracks in the formations."

Once they'd completely cleared the portal, Walter showed Cloyd how to rig his headlamp and how to ignite the gas that came from the water dripping on the carbide. Then they started inside.

As they ventured down the center of the narrow railway, the air felt pleasantly cool. Cloyd glanced constantly over his shoulder to the blinding white light of the portal; he banged his hard hat against a tooth of rock in the low ceiling. The cold surprised him, suddenly finding his bones. Next time he'd wear his sweatshirt and jacket. At the end of the tunnel, he was surprised by the ore car, big enough that both of them could have climbed in. "How'd you get this thing up here?" he asked.

"Oh, I had to take it apart with the torch and whatnot, machine new parts for bolting it back together, bring it in pieces up here on horseback, then reassemble it. The rails were somethin' else again."

In the morning they entered the mine ready for work. Cloyd held tight to the heavy drill bits and the long copper spoons. The one thing he liked was the feel of the hard hat and the hiss of burning gas in his headlamp. Before long, he told himself, he'd be accustomed to the strangeness inside the mountain. Working with the old man he wouldn't be so afraid of being trapped in the dark under the earth. At the end of the tunnel, Walter pointed out the vein of silver ore he'd been following many years before on his way to the gold contact. Cloyd was surprised to find it wasn't silver-colored at all, but black, peppered here and there in the quartz.

"Now set those spoons and drills down," Walter said. "I'll tell you how we're going to start. We'll drill seven lucky holes in a circle around this vein, then three in the center about two feet apart in a triangle, anglin' 'em so they meet inside like the top of a pyramid."

"Then the dynamite?"

"Not yet. We drill a reliever at the top of the face, edgers on both sides, and a lifter at the bottom. If we do it right, we time the charges so the center comes out first, making space so's everything around it has somewhere to go when it's blasted a hair later. The lifter going last kicks it all out where we can muck it into the ore car."

"What do I do?"

"You're my partner when we're double-jackin'. That's one man working the drill bit, the other the sledgehammer. We'll stop every so often and fish out the dust with the spoons."

"How fast can we go?" Cloyd asked with little hope.

"Not fast at all. But what's time to a hog? I'll tell you what a good pace would be, though, so you know what those old-timers could do. A good pair of double-jackers could drill two inches a minute if they were going all out. Over a longer run, like an hour, they'd go maybe thirty inches."

"Why can't we?"

"We've got to play it safe. We're two days from help. Those drill heads make a mighty small target for a sledgehammer. Once I saw a Fourth of July drillin' contest up in Silverton that really made an impression on me—now this is a true story. The object of the competition was to see how deep you could drill in fifteen minutes. These two bull-strong Cornishmen took their turn havin' at a six-foot-thick slab of Gunnison granite. The man on the sledge, early on in the contest, he's working at a good fifty-blow-per-minute pace. Of a sudden we see his hammer stopped up in the air. We realize he's just hit his partner's hand,

and the crowd groans, but the hurt man yells, 'Bring it down! Bring it down!'"

"What did that mean?"

"He didn't want to quit even though he'd been hurt bad. So the sledgeman resumes hammering. We see the hand go red, the man's face showin' it's all he can do to keep the bit turning. His blood is mixing with the water flushin' out the dust. Every time the hammer comes down, the crowd is splashed with bloody water. Then it's time for the hurt man to take his turn with the sledge, and still he won't quit. When the hammer's up in the air, the blood runs down his arm until it's red all the way to the shoulder. That man never gave up until the timer gave the signal. Then he fainted dead away."

"He died?"

"No—blacked out."

"Did they win?"

"No," Walter said thoughtfully, "they didn't come close. But they finished. Couldn't pay men to do that no more. Then again, there's fools like us doing it for free!"

To Cloyd it all seemed impossibly strange and dangerous. But he would work. If he worked as hard as he had making the fenceline, he wouldn't feel the strangeness or the danger. And this time he'd trust in the old man and not blow up like before.

After seven days of bone-rattling drilling they were ready to blast. As Walter wished, Cloyd waited outside while he placed the dynamite in the drill holes and set the timing on the fuses.

Cloyd was exhausted. The cold had sapped all his

strength. The work had been repetitive, painful, end-less. In a pretty place he could enjoy working; in the mine he'd endured it only for the sake of the old man. At first they'd taken long breaks outside, down by the creek where they could lie in the grass, eat, and rest. But as the days went by, Walter stretched the working hours and made the breaks shorter. Close to the blasting, Cloyd could tell the old man didn't want to break at all or even sleep. He was so excited, he wanted to work through to the end to see what he would find.

At last all was ready. Walter came out of the mine to make sure Cloyd was standing well clear of the portal, then went back inside to set off the charges. After awhile he came running out of the tunnel with a wild look in his eye, and yelled, "Fire in the hole! Fire in the hole!"

Cloyd smiled. The expression on the old man's face made it all worthwhile. Then came the waves of concussion as the charges rumbled inside the mine and dark clouds of smoke and dust poured out the entrance.

It was some time before the air cleared enough for them to reenter the mine. Cloyd was surprised to see how little progress the blast had made. No more than four feet. Walter knelt and examined piece after piece of the rock freed by the explosion. He'd hoped there might be at least some good silver ore for them to take home, but he was disappointed. "Poor makin's," he said. "Weak silver. Not even worth packing out for assay."

They had nothing to show for their long days, Cloyd thought. But then, he'd never really believed they'd find anything. Now they'd have to shovel all the broken rock into the car and drop it over the edge of the dump outside. It would take many loads to clear out the tunnel for work on the next round. Yet Walter turned to the hand-mucking with new enthusiasm. "Next time we'll turn up something better," he said. "We're after gold anyway. You talk to that lucky bear of yours. This is still a promising vein, and silver can lead to gold."

Cloyd was convinced they were wasting their time, but he said nothing. He'd been trying to hide his feelings from the old man. Somehow there hadn't been any time for him to go fishing. Somehow, after the first few nights, there was no time set aside to sit around the campfire in the evenings. There'd only been time to work, eat, and sleep.

Shovelful by weary shovelful, he helped Walter muck out the tunnel. The bigger rocks he had to grapple with and lift by hand. Once the ore car was finally filled, they had to wedge its wheels to a stop every few feet, or it would speed out of control and hurtle over the dump down to the creek.

Each night, he'd noticed, the cold seemed to bite a little deeper. The fragile high-country summer was beginning to lose out to winter. He fretted that he was losing his chance at the peaks. It took them a whole day to clear the mine. The prospect of starting all over again on the next round of drilling was worse than the work itself. Six or seven more days of spine-wracking torment to endure before they'd be ready to blast again. Before long, he knew too well, they'd have to leave the mountains, and then school would start. His precious time in the mountains was being used to take the inside of one apart and move it outside.

He was trying hard, but he wasn't sure he'd be able
to hold up.

Three, four, five days of the second go-round passed.
Cloyd worked in a trance, trying to concentrate on
turning the bit between blows. There was only the
penetrating cold and the hiss of burning acetylene in
his headlamp, the numbing feel of cold steel in his
hands, the stinging shock of the blow, and the harsh
reports of the hammer rattling up and down the con-
fines of the mine. It was enough to drive him crazy.

More and more, Walter begrudged himself the time
it took to eat and sleep. He had to see what the next
blast would turn up. He'd come up with fresh calcu-
lations and convinced himself he was closer than he'd
thought to the contact, that artery of high-grade gold
ore which would lead him directly to the heart of the
mountain. His old obsession had taken over and he'd
forgotten about the boy, about Cloyd's great desire to
see the high country. He'd forgotten what he told Susan James, that the trip wasn't so much for the mining
as the chance to introduce the boy to the mountains.

Though it had lain dormant for almost forty years,
the great illness of his youth—gold fever—had blos-
somed in its most virulent strain and invaded all his
faculties. He'd slipped into the assumption that their
enterprise was as exciting for Cloyd as it was for himself. Until, that is, they neared the second round of
blasting. In a moment of clarity during their midday
break he happened to read the boy's face. He realized
he'd made the boy a prisoner of sorts again and must
set him free at once. But he had to do it in such a way
that Cloyd wouldn't feel compelled to stay and help

out. He himself had no intention of quitting with the contact so near.

A stratagem came to mind. Not one his wife would have approved of, or he either under ordinary circumstances. It deviated by a substantial margin from the truth. A white lie, he told himself, for the boy's benefit. "Well, Cloyd, I've had it," he said disgustedly.

Surprised, Cloyd looked up and saw the disappointment all across the old man's face. "How do you mean?" he asked.

"Like they say in the oil business, it's a dry hole. We're wasting our time."

"But you won't know until you blow it up again and see."

A logical objection, Walter thought. He'd have to counter with bogus expertise. "Oh, I've been looking at the powder we've been fishing out of the drill holes with those spoons. Indications are bad, mighty poor. I figure we ought to give it up before we shoot what's left of the summer. Didn't you want to climb one of these mountains, maybe that Rio Grande Pyramid?"

"Maybe the gold's just a little farther," Cloyd insisted.

"Maybe. But chances are slim to none. If we quit now we'll have a little time—maybe a week—before we have to head back. Now what about that Pyramid? Let's get you some food packed, go over some maps— why, you could be ready to take out in the morning."

"Aren't you coming with me?"

For a moment, Walter was so touched that Cloyd would want him along, he almost abandoned his plan. Though he lacked the wind for climbing at high altitude, they could ride together and set up a base camp before the boy set out alone. But even more he was relishing the next blast and the treasure it might break loose. "My lungs couldn't take the thin air," he said. "That's close to fourteen thousand feet. I might have a fit or somethin'."

"We wouldn't have to go so high up."

"No, Cloyd, I'd rather stick close to camp here and just enjoy myself pokin' around, lookin' at the scenery, brewin' coffee and whatnot. You take Blueboy—you're better off on horseback as far as you can go. Take a packhorse too. Park your horses in the trees before you climb up above timberline."

Suddenly Walter was spooked. He shouldn't be letting the boy go off alone in the mountains. It was never a good idea, no matter how experienced you were. Yet he'd done it often enough when he was young. "Stay off of those peaks when the weather's comin' on. You know what that's about."

"I'll be careful," Cloyd promised.

16

Mile by mile Cloyd rode up the gentle meadows of the Pine. As he saw the Rio Grande Pyramid gradually nearing, his confidence grew. He rode with beauty all around him. He rode on a powerful horse who was his friend. "Hey-a, Blueboy, hey-a!"

Cloyd's spirit was free and had all the running room in the world. There was no limit to where it might go or what was possible. "Hey-a," he sang. "Hey-a, hey-a, Blueboy."

The roan tried to break into a trot, even into a run, but the packhorse held him back. Cloyd could tell that Blueboy was taken with the morning's wild spirit; this day was made for the two of them. He dismounted and tied the packhorse to a tree, a little ways off the trail, and then he walked back to the roan and said,

"Let's run, Blue, I mean really run."

And then they ran streaming through the meadows of the Pine. Cloyd and the horse were one, and they were flying through the wind and the light, while all around him shone the mountains and the trees and the river. Cloyd grinned as they ran, and then he broke into a smile. His teeth caught the wind. He couldn't stop smiling all the way up the meadow. This day was different. It was as if he was coming into a new world all bright and shining, and it was made for him.

They rested at the end of the meadow, and they drank from the stream. The roan was delighted with the meadow grass and tore at it as if he hadn't eaten for weeks. Cloyd lay on his back in the grass and watched the trees on the hillside sway in the wind. He wondered if trees could feel. He decided that they could. They liked to wrap themselves in the air, sway with the breeze, and let the air soothe their branches and every little needle.

Back on the horse, he leaned forward to speak. The roan swiveled an ear back. "Want to?" Cloyd whispered. "Want to, Blue?"

The roan exploded into a gallop, and they ran all the way back down the meadow. Then he collected the packhorse and continued on his way to the Pyramid. After several miles he had to leave the trail and strike upward through the dark spruce forest. There were no trails where he was going. Blueboy and the packhorse labored in the rapidly thinning air as Cloyd guided them through the deadfall. Up, up they climbed. After a few miles Cloyd rested them on a bench where waterfalls spilled into a string of beaver ponds. The horses grazed while Cloyd ate his lunch. Contentment seeped through and through him. This place was almost enough, he felt so good. The peak, if he made it, would be surplus to store against the future. He resolved to see as much of the mountains as he could. Besides the Pyramid, he was taken with two other names: Ute Lake and the Rincon La Osa, "the corner of the bear."

As he climbed again, the spruces huddled in clusters, squatter than they grew below, and grassy slopes led to a world of wildflowers. He left the last of the trees behind and rode through windblown waves of reds, yellows, and blues. He could almost reach out and touch the Continental Divide. That's where, as Walter had explained, rivers bound for different oceans started out within spitting distance of each other.

He rested the horses while he took it all in. Here he was in the high, treeless world patched with snowbanks as far as he could see, the spongy, delicate, windlashed birthplace of rivers. A lone giant, the Pyramid loomed above and only a few miles away. He wondered if it could really be climbed. Close at hand, a spectacular formation in the Divide caught his fancy. It was called the Window, and it was so close he could see birds flying in the wide gap between its sheer walls. They were small birds, and they seemed to be flying loops for the sheer joy of it. They come to play, he realized. The air must pour through there like anything.

He noticed a bit of an elk trail leading to the Window across the steep scree slides of fine rock. On the spur of the moment he said to the roan, "You want to stand in that Window, Blueboy? I sure do." He tied the packhorse and rode the roan toward the Window. He wanted to stand between those towering walls and feel the air currents, see the birds up close, and look over the other side.

They started across the elk trail. Once out on the scree slope, Cloyd thought the elk that cross it must be very surefooted, or very brave. The fine rock slid under the roan's hoofs, and the steepness of the slope underneath them began to worry him. Maybe it's a mountain goat trail, he thought. Yet there was no place to turn around, no choice but to keep going forward.

They inched across the dizzying slope until they reached the Window, and then the roan balked about going up. "We're almost there," Cloyd encouraged him. Then he chuckled, and said, "Don't you want to stand on that windowsill?" With a jump, the roan gained the rock ledge and they were standing right where Cloyd wanted to be, in between those sheer walls like towers. He watched the swallows put on a show. He could even see the rainbow in their wing patches. To the north, across the Rio Grande country, a whole new world had opened up. It seemed like the wilderness had no end.

If only the old man could see us standing here, he thought—me and Blueboy in the Window. I wish my sister could, my grandmother, and Susan James. But especially the old man. What a wonderful day, he thought. And there's not a cloud in the sky.

Cloyd thought about the Pyramid. There was still time to climb it today. Tomorrow the weather could turn bad.

He realized it would be harder for the roan to step off the windowsill than it had been to scramble up. He could fall. Besides, he liked the idea of riding *through* the Window, and so he did. He rode through, and then he looped one of the towers until he gained the ridgetop and picked up a thread of a trail. The slope was awful steep, but it wasn't all scree like the one he crossed before; there was quite a bit of grass on it. Halfway down, the roan pulled up and held his ground. In front of them, a spring popped out of the mountain and made a little bog on the slope. Cloyd didn't know why the roan wouldn't go across. The horse was looking around, but there was no passage above or below the muddy spot. "We don't mind the mud," Cloyd said. He smacked his lips and kicked the horse forward. "C'mon, Blueboy, you can do it. You can do it, Blueboy."

The roan tried the mud and eased into it. Afterward, Cloyd remembered how the horse glanced back at him, as if for reassurance.

The roan took another step and was into the mud all the way up to one of his front shoulders. His other three legs were scrambling, scrambling desperately for footing, but the one leg was trapped, and Blueboy was falling.

In the moment the horse went down, it was all a blur. Cloyd knew only that he was about to be crushed. He barely managed to free his feet from the stirrups and to lunge uphill as the roan fell on its side.

Cloyd was pinned in the mud, and all around his head were the four hoofs of the roan. He saw the horseshoes and even the nails in the horseshoes.

Cloyd saw Blueboy tense and prepare to kick. The

roan had to kick for balance, to resist the pull of the slope underneath him, and when he did, he'd crush the boy's skull. Cloyd thrashed with all his might to free himself, but he was completely mired.

Their eyes met, in a moment Cloyd would never forget. Blueboy was poised to kick, and then he saw Cloyd's head there, and then he didn't kick, not at all, but slowly, slowly, rolled over on his back. All four legs arced away from the boy, and then Blueboy tucked his legs in and tumbled down the mountain, slowly at first, then faster and faster like a trundling boulder.

The roan lay at the foot of the scree slope several hundred feet below. Full of dread, Cloyd freed himself from the mud and worked his way down to the horse. Blueboy was alive, but how badly hurt? His breathing came in spurts; he wasn't getting up. "Maybe you're okay," he told the horse, without believing it might be so. "Maybe you're okay. You gotta get up! Are your legs broken? Are you all busted up inside?"

Cloyd made the roan stand up. He was amazed to see Blueboy get up and then walk. He kept talking to the horse; he was so relieved and thankful. After a little while, he led Blueboy down to the tundra grass. Somehow, there were no broken bones, nothing to show but a few scratches. Somehow, they'd both lived through it. He led the horse down and around the base of the slope and back up to the packhorse.

Cloyd found a camp barely into the trees, by a trickle of a stream running off the snowbanks. There was no way he was going to try to climb the Pyramid this day. Brushing the dried mud off his clothes, he marveled at the sacrifice his horse had made. He shouldn't have taken Blueboy where he did. He wondered if he would climb the Pyramid at all; he wondered if he should even try. Maybe he should just get back to the old man while he was safe. He didn't really know what he was doing anyway. He'd almost killed the horse, could've got killed himself. What did he need to stand on the top of a mountain for anyway? Cloyd brooded through the long evening, finally crawled into his sleeping bag, and fell asleep by the fading fire. In his dreams, the horse kept falling over and over all night. He woke up, freezing in the cold night air. He should have pitched his tent. He wished the day would come.

At first light he woke, and he knew he couldn't ride away and give up, leave his dream behind. Maybe he would fail, but at least he had to try. Maybe what happened with the roan was all a part of earning the peak, not a reason to give up. Hadn't the old man said that the hurt you get over makes you stronger?

He ate quickly and set out on foot. "Good-bye, Blueboy," he called over his shoulder. "I'm going for the top of the world."

Within a few hours he'd angled up the mountain far enough to emerge from the trees and find the Pyramid towering right in front of him. As yet not a cloud had formed over the mountains. Already he could see the mesas down in New Mexico. How much greater would be the view from the peak, where he would be able to see in all directions. With spirits rising he bounded from rock to rock on the talus slopes tumbling from the ridge high above. The small rock-rabbits called pikas squeaked and scurried among the boulders on all sides. A marmot the size of a small dog stood on its hind legs and whistled shrilly at him. He grinned to think about how the old man called them whistle pigs. "Are you a whistle pig?" he asked playfully. The marmot whistled once more. "I guess you are. I wish I could whistle like that."

Clouds were forming quickly up and down the range as he reached the mountain. He could imagine what a lightning storm on the peak would be like; he wasted no time picking a route. There was only one by which he had a chance of reaching the summit, and that was the knife-edge in front of him where two planes of the Pyramid met. He left the pikas and the marmots behind and started picking his way up the knife-edge. Now it was all rock. Some of the rocks were loose and could take him with them. A fall down either face would be deadly, but the north side would be the worst. He'd slide a thousand feet on the snow before being pitched onto the boulders below.

Cloyd kept climbing and tried to keep his mind on each step, each handhold. The air was thin and seared his lungs. Every time he reached a spot that might have stopped him, he found a way around or located cracks and footholds that enabled him to continue. The clouds were building and starting to darken, but they were still in the distance. Cloyd felt strong. He remembered that first day at the old man's farm when he climbed to the outcrop, found the bearstone, and fastened his longing on these peaks. He fell into the rhythm of climbing and proceeded up the knife-edge at a steady, careful pace.

A calm joy lifted Cloyd up the final piece of the climb. He was as sure he'd make the top as he'd ever been of anything. He seemed to float up the last little bit and stepped to the very tip of the Pyramid.

Peaks on all sides were riding in the blue sky. Peaks everywhere, dancing, jutting up, all in motion. He had to sit down and grip the rock. Peaks, as far as he could see, peaks, rock and green tundra, snow banks, spruce forests, river canyons.

As he caught his breath, Cloyd saw a big bird soaring far below. Probably it was an eagle. He enjoyed its mastery of the winds, then watched it disappear. A storm was gathering in the Needles, and shadows were overtaking the mountainsides. Out in the low country, the sun was still shining. He was amazed to recognize the Chuska Mountains in the hazy distance. They were the same mountains he always saw from White Mesa. Home wasn't really so far away. Someday he'd go home, he knew, but it didn't have to be soon. Whenever it happened would be all right. Cloyd pulled the blue stone from his pocket and set the little bear on a flat rock at the very top of the mountain. "Lone Bear," he said aloud, "we're not so alone anymore."

Cloyd thought about how Walter liked to be deep in the cold darkness of his gold mine. He wished the old man could have stood here with him. He wanted to tell him *this* is the heart of the mountains, up here in the light where you can see forever. Where you feel like you're a part of it all, like the beating heart of the mountains is your own heart. He'd never felt this way before, free and peaceful at the same time. If only there was a way to show the old man how thankful he was, for this, for Blueboy, for everything. He could show he cared for Walter like a son for a father.

The wind began to blow hard, and the temperature

was dropping. He'd have to start down soon. He wished he could stay longer and try to take it all in, but it didn't matter. He had fulfilled his dream. It would be something he could always keep with him.

Then he remembered what his grandmother had told him, how the Utes knew all these mountains. Other Utes like himself must have stood on this same peak years ago. They had probably done something special, said or sung something. Then Cloyd recalled a ceremony his grandmother had taught him, but which he'd never done. Taking the bearstone in his hand, he held it out and offered it in turn to the Four Directions, then to the Earth and the Sky.

17

Cloyd was eager now to be on his way back to the old man. But he wouldn't take the shortest way; there was more he wanted to see. Dropping through the deep timber, he picked up the Divide trail and followed it until he sighted Ute Lake, a deep green crater tucked under the north slope at timberline.

On the way down he saw three bull elk grazing in the lush grass along a rivulet that fed the lake. When they heard the horse coming down the switchbacks, the elk hurried up the far side of the basin and into the brushy mountain willows beyond.

At lakeside, Cloyd made his camp and hobbled his horses in the good grass. Before long he had his rod and reel assembled and was searching for bait. He found a tiny grasshopper and dropped it on the surface of the deep and rocky lake, but the fish weren't interested. They could see its legs kicking, but they weren't interested. He tried the salmon eggs. No luck. The trout started hitting the surface for flies even tiner than gnats. He wondered if the old Utes had fished at this lake named after them, and how. He laughed out loud. He doubted they were fly fishermen.

As the sun was dropping behind the Needles, he sat by his fire and ate a chili supper. It tasted good, and the packhorse would have one less can to carry. Warmth and contentment spread through his body.

Cloyd's fourth morning found him riding out of Ute Lake up to the Divide and descending into the long alpine basin called the Rincon La Osa, which would lead him back to the valley of the Pine. This night he'd be at the mine with Walter, he thought happily. He thought about how he was going to tell the old man about that moment when his eyes and Blueboy's met, that he'd found out the answer to the question of whether horses could care about you. The red-haired man was wrong about horses, at least about this one. He had a lot he wanted to talk about with Walter. He wondered if Walter would recognize how much he'd grown in four days' time.

He stopped to rest and eat berries on the bank of the Rincon stream as it wound its way slowly across a small meadow below the long basin. Kneeling by the stream to drink, he marveled at the clarity of the water, which seemed to magnify every pebble on the bottom. He became aware that he was looking as well at the dark backs of three large trout, motionless except for the fanning of their fins.

One of them, perhaps becoming aware of him,

darted up a tiny inlet on his side of the creek. Cloyd followed and kept his eye on the fish moving slowly up the narrow passage. He'd like to catch this fish, he thought, catch it somehow without a fishing pole. Was it true what his grandmother had said, that in the old days some of the Utes could catch fish in their bare hands?

He would try. The fish would have to come back to the stream sometime. He could pick a spot and wait for it to come through.

With one knee on each bank, Cloyd straddled the inlet. Slowly he lowered his hands and then his arms into the icy water as deep as his arms were long. And then he waited.

Five minutes, ten minutes, he couldn't tell anymore. His arms went numb, his back ached, but he didn't move a muscle. He could see the trout slowly swimming toward him, pausing here and there for long minutes.

The trout was close now. Cloyd could see its mouth working, its bright orange markings. It was looking through the tunnel his hands and arms made. Would it retreat or dart between his hands before he could close on it? He held them as still as he could. It swam still closer. He began to narrow the gap between his freezing hands, slowly, slowly, slowly. Unsuspecting, the cutthroat swam between them. Cloyd closed in as calmly as he could. He dug with his nails, grasped the fish, and lifted it in one motion out of the water and onto the bank.

He stood up to ease the striking pain in his back. The horses whinnied. A dark shape was moving at the edge of the meadow. An animal loping with an unusual gait. A bear! A huge brown bear, and it was aware of him. It stood on its hind legs to have a look at him, and its head swayed back and forth. Cloyd was astonished at how tall it was. Its claws were enormous. The bear dropped quickly to all fours and suddenly disappeared into the trees.

The big fish flip-flopped against Cloyd's leg. He nudged it back into the water with his foot, then leaped across the Rincon stream and took off running in hopes of a second glimpse of the huge bear. Once in the trees Cloyd walked softly, looking all around, and tried to listen for the bear's passage. All he could hear was the furious pounding of his own heart.

In the quiet darkness of the trees, the bear was nowhere and everywhere. Suddenly Cloyd felt foolish and reckless for having tried to follow. He ran back to the sunlit meadow, to the horses. He wanted to hurry back to the camp on Snowslide Creek. He wanted to tell the old man about the bear.

It was late afternoon when he rode into camp. He was anxious to see Walter. The old man was drinking coffee and visiting by the campfire with his friend Rusty, the red-haired man.

Walter's face lit up when he saw Cloyd. "I didn't expect you until tomorrow or so," he said. "How'd everything go?"

"Fine," Cloyd mumbled. All his enthusiasm was squelched. The tall man was looking him over, like he did before. No handshake this time, but all the feelings were the same as before.

"Cloyd here's been out exploring the mountains. Did you climb that Rio Grande Pyramid?"

Cloyd nodded halfheartedly. He felt so disappointed

that someone else was there, and worse, that it was the red-haired man. This wasn't how it was supposed to be.

"My goodness, that must've been something. I'll bet you could see hundreds of miles from up there."

"See any wildlife?" the outfitter asked abruptly.

Cloyd's heart began to pound. This wasn't as he'd pictured it, telling Walter how he'd caught the fish and seen the bear. But the outfitter had brought the subject up, and the man was making him feel bad again, sick even, as if he was suddenly burning up with fever. He cast wildly about thinking for what to say or do, but he couldn't think; he could only feel the resentment burning inside, and he wanted to prove himself, show that he wasn't a nothing, show that he knew something, something that would impress the big hunter. He'd seen a bear without having had to track it down with dogs. "Some elk . . ." he said, teetering on the brink, and then he added, " . . . and a bear."

"When'd you see the bear?" the man asked quickly.

"Today."

"What kind?"

Cloyd hesitated. "He was brown. I guess he was a brown bear."

"No such varmint. Black bear in a cinnamon phase. How big?"

"Taller than you, standing up."

The red-haired man smiled condescendingly. "Me standing up, you say, or the bear?"

"Both."

The man grunted. "You saw this bear standing on its hind legs? How far away was he?"

Now Cloyd regretted he'd said anything at all. Suddenly he didn't feel good about seeing the bear. The man was making him feel bad, making it seem in front of Walter like he was exaggerating. Maybe he was, a little, but he really didn't think so. What could he do now? He saw what he saw, and he wouldn't let the tall man shame him. "Just across the meadow," he said.

The man lifted his red eyebrows. "Oh, whereabouts?"

Again he hesitated. "Rincon," he said finally.

"Oh? La Vaca or La Osa?"

"La Osa."

"Rincon of the Bear, eh?" he said skeptically, with a wide grin. "Walter, you think he might've let his imagination get away from him up in that high altitude?"

Agitated, Walter got up. The conversation had gone badly. Cloyd had been embarrassed. His friend had no feel for the boy at all. "Why no, Rusty," he declared, "that ain't possible. Cloyd's got an eye for detail better'n mine by far."

The tall man rose, hung his coffee cup in the branch of a tree, and crossed the fire circle to Cloyd. He clapped Cloyd's shoulder. "No hard feelings, kid. I believed every word you said. I'm just part lawyer, I guess, and curious to boot. Say, I've got to be going, Walter—my brothers are expecting me for supper."

Walter put together a meal for the boy. They ate quietly. Walter didn't pester him; he could see Cloyd didn't want to talk just now. Walter let his mind drift, mulling things over. Like about how he'd been single-jacking all this time the boy was gone, day and night practically, when he'd told the boy he wouldn't. He was nearly ready to fire and should be getting some sleep, lest he make a mistake during the crucial preparation of the charges.

Cloyd's grown, Walter reflected. He's stronger, more like a young man than a boy. Because of how it went with Rusty, he'd have to wait awhile before asking Cloyd about the ride. They should've shared the ride in the first place. On the other hand, sometimes it was better to be out there on your own. That's when you really see things and learn something. Cloyd got to have the whole country to himself.

Tomorrow he'd fire the hole. Funny, it didn't really matter if he found anything. How could he expect to with only two blasts? That wasn't a significant amount of progress. But it was the trying again that made it worthwhile. This round might be his last ever. All his steels were dull, and it wouldn't do any good to try to sharpen them anymore—they needed retempering. The summer was run out anyway. His life, for that matter, was about run. But he'd come back to the Pride of the West the way he'd always wanted to, come full circle.

There was something weighing in the air tonight, Walter thought, something weighing on this time that should be savored. As he watched the boy in the firelight, he saw it building. Maybe Cloyd, too, was realizing that the summer was about over. It wouldn't do any good to talk about it. There'd be time yet for ending on the upside.

It was Cloyd who broke the long silence. "Why did he keep asking me about that bear I saw?"

"How do you mean?"

"He didn't believe me."

"Oh, he was trying to pick your memory."

Cloyd shook his head decisively. "He wanted to catch me saying something that wasn't right so he could prove I was making it up."

"Oh, no. I know Rusty awful well. He was so interested he could hardly hold himself still. Didn't you see how fast he took off? He was bustin' to get back to camp and get started after that bear. Sounded like a trophy."

Cloyd struggled against the panic that ripped him. His breath caught short, and his heart pounded in his ears. "It's not hunting season," he said, as calmly as he could. "Bear season was in June, wasn't it?"

"Open season on bears, Cloyd, or there's hunts off and on all year, I forget which."

Cloyd's mind raced. He'd given away the bear, and the outfitter was going to try to kill it. "Does he have those dogs with him?"

"They don't use any on this hunt. Too easy, they say. You see, Rusty and his brothers get together every summer for a pleasure-hunt. It's kind of a contest. The first brother to get himself a bear wins a prize of some kind."

"They can find a bear without dogs?"

"They're awful good. Rusty's the best trapper, tracker, and hunter in the San Juans. As a matter of fact, they're bowhunting."

"What do you mean?"

"Why, with bows and arrows. That's the way Rusty favors. He even writes articles for a magazine about bowhunting."

"There was a rifle in the case on his horse."

"Well, he'd have it along with him. But he prefers to bowhunt because it takes quite a bit more skill. It's like the Indians used to, only the arrows are made out of fiberglass or some-such and the head's like three razor blades in one. You wouldn't want to touch the thing—it'd take your thumb off. Even so, the odds against the hunter getting close enough are pretty long. Sometimes these guys come up empty-handed. Take this hunt for instance. They'll be heading back sometime soon and still have nothing to show. They probably won't come within miles of that bear of yours. Bears cover a lot of ground, you know. The chances of finding any one bear with that kind of head start are slim at best."

Cloyd wasn't reassured. The old man said the outfitter was the best trapper, tracker, and hunter in the mountains. This man might very well kill the bear, and he'd told him where to find it. Now he'd done it, spoiled everything. In the old days, his grandmother said, the Utes wouldn't kill bears. That would bring on the worst of bad luck, she said. Cloyd considered his secret name and fingered the bearstone in his pocket. He had to undo his mistake.

18

Cloyd hoped to slip out of camp as soon as the moon rose to light his way. He struggled to stay awake after Walter fell asleep, but soon failed, worn out by his long ride off the Divide. The moon was high in the sky when he awoke. He feared that the red-haired man had already gone up the Rincon after the bear. The old man's breathing whistled its usual song; Cloyd was able to collect his jacket and slide through the tent flap without waking him.

He climbed in the moonlight to a vantage point above the confluence of the Rincon creek and the Pine River, and waited, his confidence collapsing all around him. He was alarmed by every sound the night made.

To his relief, he finally spotted the outfitter riding up the Pine trail. It was still all but dark, yet Cloyd recognized the profile of the tall man. He wondered why the man was alone, then recalled the contest among the brothers. The outfitter wanted the bear all for himself.

In the first light the outfitter trotted his horse along the flats at the bottom of the Rincon creek. From the point the man disappeared into the trees, the trail climbed so abruptly that his horse would be slowed to a walk. Cloyd ran to keep up. He wished he had Blueboy, but a horse would give him away turning over stones and breaking sticks. He had to follow so carefully that the best tracker in the mountains wouldn't know he was being followed.

Maybe the bear's gone over the mountains, Cloyd hoped, across the rockslides where even the red-haired man couldn't track him. But what if he had just killed a deer and would stay in the Rincon to feed a few days? What if he's eating berries along the stream in the meadow?

Cloyd hurried up the mountain, cutting the switchbacks and watching to make sure he didn't come too close to the man on horseback. Finally he could see through the trees to the meadow, the one where he'd seen the bear. He stopped to take off his jacket. He'd soaked himself with sweat. The outfitter, he guessed, was even now on the meadow looking for signs. Cloyd crawled to the edge of the trees and peeked around the trunk of a large spruce.

He saw the horse first, then the man kneeling in the grass where the bear had loped toward the trees and stood up. It hadn't taken the tall man much time to find the track of the bear. He was as skillful as Walter said, and after all, Cloyd thought bitterly, he'd been told right where to go.

As eager as he might be, the red-haired man took his time examining the signs, especially around the place where the bear stood up. Then he climbed the tongue of a talus slide to a spot well above the meadow where he crouched awhile and scanned in all directions with his large binoculars.

In a bowl like this any sound would carry, Cloyd knew, yet the outfitter descended the slope as quietly as a cat. He's hunting, Cloyd realized—he's deadly serious. Cloyd remembered how the red-haired man had almost laughed at him. If the man knew, he would simply sneer at the suggestion that an unarmed boy on foot hoped to stop him.

How could it be done? Maybe make enough noise to warn the bear? That's what he'd been thinking as he rushed up the trail. But if he yelled and scared the bear away, wouldn't the man catch up again? How could the bear escape the best tracker in the country?

Cloyd watched the man return to the signs on the meadow. Most likely he hadn't caught sight of the bear through the binoculars.

The outfitter packed a daypack with his binoculars and what must have been food and water. Cloyd watched him string his bow and check his arrows one by one. How close would you have to get, Cloyd wondered, to hunt with a bow and arrow? The man hobbled his horse, entered the trees where the bear had, and disappeared.

The man's rifle must be in the saddle scabbard on the horse, Cloyd reasoned. With the rifle he could make plenty of noise. The mountains would echo the shots all the way to the bear, wherever it was.

The rifle was there in the scabbard, as he'd hoped. But when Cloyd pulled the bolt back and exposed the chamber, there was no ammunition in it. He searched the saddlebags—no shells! The outfitter must have them in his daypack. The man was gone now, the chance to keep him in sight lost.

Cloyd knew he lacked the skill to track the man or the bear in the woods. His only chance now was to get back to the trees on the other side of the meadow, on the slope opposite the one the man was on. That way he could climb without being seen and find a high place where he might spot the outfitter again—if he was lucky.

Cloyd worked for most of an hour until he found a lookout close to timberline, high above the dogleg between the lower and upper meadows. Great ups and downs rippled the upper basin, where even now the outfitter or the bear or both might be hidden from view. Big patches of stunted spruce dotted the flanks of the basin, and thickets of brush grew everywhere, looking from this distance like tall grass. A thousand places he couldn't see. I'm an unlucky person, he thought.

Cloyd can't be too far off, Walter thought. He didn't take the horse. He'll be back. Walter's mind drifted back to his work, as he readied the charges for the second blast. Once you blast, he reflected, you forget about all the backbreaking work. Another three or four feet of the mountain is broken loose, and you just never know what you're going to find. Most times nothing but rock. A bonanza, he mused, is a hole in the ground owned by a champion liar. But sometimes a man found good ore, and once in a million lifetimes, a fabulous strike like the Cresson Vug. It's really gambling, is what it is, he thought. They ought to make it illegal.

Walter came running out of the tunnel hollering, "Fire in the hole! Fire in the hole!" even though there was no one to hear it but himself. Muffled somewhat, the blast sent fewer clouds of fumes and dust than usual out of the mouth of the mine. He was concerned that the explosion lacked punch. When the air cleared enough for him to see, he entered the mine. So what if the air's still bad, he thought. No sense in an old man babying his lungs.

He groaned when he saw the blasted face at the end of the tunnel, recognizing at once what was wrong. The old face had been only partially blown out; two mounds of rock held the bulk of it fast. Two missed shots—worse than rotten luck. Two mounds of rock clinging there with crucial charges inside, unshot but possibly hair-triggered to blow when a man tried to pick at the surrounding rock to get at them.

Outside, he sat and thought about the missed shots. He could wait until next summer to try to pick them out, but then they'd be hanging over his head all winter and he'd still have to face them. He could give up on the Pride of the West, he supposed. But one thing he couldn't do—wait until somebody was blown up fooling around inside the mine. If he was going to remove them, he'd better try while he had the nerve and while the boy was safely away blowing off steam. "Maude, you were right—it's a risky business," he said aloud.

He lit the headlamp, shouldered the pick, and entered the tunnel. More than anything, he had to know if the missed shots hid some decent ore.

19

The hours of careful waiting and watching ended as the tall white clouds turned dark and the wind began to blow. Cloyd glimpsed a figure moving swiftly for a low spot several miles up the basin. If it was the man on the track of the bear, it meant the bear had moved up the Rincon in the direction of the Divide.

Cloyd took off running. He avoided the meadows and tried to make time in the stands of timber and in the brush. He glimpsed the figure again clearing the top of the Divide, vanishing just as lightning struck up there. Apparently the outfitter had dropped his tracking and hurried up the ridge while Cloyd was in the brush. The man was taking a risk climbing into the weather, Cloyd thought. He must be closing in on the bear.

Cloyd broke into the open and made for the place where the man went over the top. As he climbed, it began to sprinkle; he had no rain gear. He ran stumbling up the ridge and into the wind with no thought but that he had to reach the bear in time.

As he topped out on the Divide, he found the outfitter's straw cowboy hat weighted and left in plain sight—as a sign for his brothers? Cloyd thought the man must be a little farther east on the Divide and a little below it. He had to be, it was the only hidden place. If he'd gone on down the steep slope to the west, he'd be visible.

The thundershower had passed by and was attacking the Pyramid. The day was waning now; he knew he had to guess right.

Yes, the outfitter had to be tucked out of sight on one of the small terraces angling to the north and dropping like stairs down to Ute Lake. The man—and the bear—must be about where he'd passed the day before on his way up from the lake.

Just in case the outfitter had somehow doubled back, Cloyd checked behind. His eye caught a flash of bright yellow. Riders in rainslickers, three of them coming up the Rincon and leading a fourth horse. The brothers. He left the ridgeline quickly.

Cloyd found the highest terrace, but the man wasn't there. He ran its length, then crawled to the far edge to avoid being seen as he gained a vantage point. Below him lay another little meadow surrounded by rockslides and brush. He made his way down to it among the rocks and ran for the far end. The wind blowing hard against him slowed him down.

When he dropped at the far end of the meadow to

look below, he saw them on the next shelf. It *was* the bear he'd seen, a huge brown bear turning over rocks above the mountain willows at the edge of the meadow, looking maybe for pikas or marmots. The outfitter was stalking in a crouch. He sneaked along the line of brush until he drew close to the bear on the other side. The man carried his bow with an arrow in place. The bear wasn't aware of him.

Cloyd yelled with all his might. Strangely, neither the bear nor the man paid any attention. The red-haired man drew close to a gap in the brushline. Cloyd screamed again and again, desperately, with no result. As close as they were, the bear and the man were deaf and unreachable, like phantoms in a dream. Then he realized that he was yelling from above and into a sturdy wind, and his voice was being blown away, up and behind him.

Suddenly the tall man stood out in the open in front of the bear with the bow pulled all the way back and the arrow aimed. Sensing something, the bear stood up as if to have a better look and took the arrow in its neck.

The bear didn't fall. It roared in pain and charged the man through the opening in the brush with uncanny speed. But the outfitter hadn't wasted any time nocking a second arrow, and released it into the bear's chest.

Still the bear came on, all teeth and claws and blood, and knocked aside the bow the man lifted to shield himself. As the man spun away, the big bear hesitated, then stood up and tried to brush away the arrowshafts with its paws.

The man crouched and brandished a long-bladed

knife. Returning to all fours, the bear took a few steps toward him, gave a strangled growl, and collapsed on its side.

The red-haired man circled the fallen bear several times. Then he knelt and ran his hand across its broad forehead. He inspected the teeth and the underside of one of the front paws, and sized the claws against his forefinger.

Cloyd fell to his belly in the cover of the rocks and let the bitterness roll over him in waves. He dreaded being seen by the outfitter now—that would make the man's victory complete. He'd gladly sink into the ground if he could. The uncaring wind shifted and carried the fragment of a shout from above and behind him. The others were coming, the brothers. He had to get out of there. He scuttled backward until he was well away from the lip of the shelf, then stood and ran off the downhill side into the rocks on the steep slope below. Above him, the riders crossed the spot he'd fled.

There was whooping and shouting as the three men met up with their brother and the dead bear, but Cloyd couldn't see them and he couldn't hear the outfitter's voice. He had to hear what the man would say. He worked his way through the talus until he was directly below them, then crept under the edge of the meadow where he could hear.

"Biggest bear I ever saw," said one. "You win again."

"You sure got the jump on us, Rusty, sneaking off in the night like that," said a second brother. "We came as soon as we saw your note. Helluva bear. Did he charge you? How'd it go?"

"Look at the forehead," the outfitter said, not so loud as the others.

"What about it?"

"It's dished out."

"So?"

"Look at the hump on its back, the forehead, the teeth, the claws—that's a grizzly."

"Everybody knows there aren't any grizzlies left in Colorado," the third brother protested.

"Wasn't true. This here's a grizzly."

"If you say so—you're the expert. Well then, you've sure got yourself a trophy here, Rusty."

"What I've got myself here is a heck of a mess."

"Waddaya mean?"

"It's illegal to kill a grizzly. They're protected. Hundred thousand dollar fine and a year in jail."

"So . . . you didn't know it was a grizzly, did you?"

"It . . . crossed my mind—I couldn't tell for sure until I was up close. . . . It charged me—I had to defend myself."

That's a lie, Cloyd thought. That's not how it happened.

"Well, who's to know?" one of the brothers snapped. "Ain't nobody's business but yours."

"I got carried away."

There was a pause, then Cloyd heard the red-haired man's voice fill with what almost seemed like regret. "It's probably one of the two cubs that were reported around the Pyramid ten or twelve years ago."

"Look, Rusty," the same brother said, "Quit worrying. You made a terrific kill here, and it'll make a once-in-a-lifetime trophy."

"You guys think I can go ahead and display it in

my home—show it to the game warden when he comes over to visit?"

"I see your point. You've got a problem here, don't you? How 'bout I just take it back to Texas with me. Let's skin it out right now."

"I don't know, Andy. I could lose my license over this—that's my livelihood we're talking about. Even if a grizzly's found dead, you're supposed to report it as soon as you can so the Department of Wildlife's scientific guys can study it."

"C'mon, we'll pack the skin out good and careful. No one'll ever see it. Tell you what. I'll give you a thousand dollars for it, make it worth your while. I'd really like to have that monster baring his teeth on the floor in front of the fireplace. Look at the size of those claws! From what you're saying, if you do report this thing, there's no way they aren't going to take it away from you. Then what if they don't like your story? You'll end up without the bear and in big trouble both!"

"We'd have to leave the carcass, Andy. Backpackers would come across it and report it. The bone structure would identify it as a grizzly. Sam Perkins—the game warden—he knows we're up here. I'd never get away with it. Besides, he's a good friend. The more I think about this, the more I'm convinced that the only way I'm going to come out at all on this deal is to get ahold of Sam right away. He's going to want to bring in the department helicopter and lift this grizzly out as soon as possible, before it starts to spoil. So let's get down to the guard station and radio this in."

"It's a helluva shame."

"Sure is," the outfitter agreed. "But I'm not going to risk my business over it."

After the men were gone, Cloyd approached the bear. Kneeling close to its massive head, Cloyd asked the bear's forgiveness. He prayed that somehow this bear wasn't the last one. Hadn't there been two cubs? Maybe there are others that nobody knows about. Overcome with grief, he stayed into darkness. Cloyd vowed to the mighty grizzly that he would remember him forever, not lifeless like now, but standing tall and alert, sniffing the wind, still the most powerful animal in the mountains.

As he fled down the Rincon trail, the night was full of accusing voices. A large owl suddenly flapped out of the dark and almost struck him. He yelled sharply in terror. His grandmother had told him about owls. This one would be the dead bear's spirit freshly loosed from its body.

20

It was no accident he'd seen the owl, Cloyd discovered. When, in the middle of the night, he stumbled into camp and lifted the flap of the canvas tent, his misgivings were verified. Instead of the musical comings and goings of the old man's breath, he was greeted by an uncanny silence. He had to fumble for a flashlight. Indeed, Walter was not there. His sleeping bag was rolled up as it always was during the day. The old man had not been to bed this night at all.

Cloyd ran up the ore dump and into the mine. His flashlight caught the trace of dust lingering in the air. There'd been a blast, he knew. And with that knowledge came the sickening realization that Walter had been working all along and had set off another round of blasting. He listened. All he could hear was the beating of his own heart. If Walter was working in there, he should be able to hear it: any sound carried in the mine. But there was no sound at all coming down the tunnel, only the uncanny silence. He called. No answer.

Cloyd found him face down at the end of the tunnel. Only the old man's head, shoulders, and right arm showed above the rubble. The explosion had made meat of one side of his face. Cloyd knelt close. Walter was still breathing, but he was unconscious. There was a nasty gash in his scalp on the back of his head, and it was all matted with blood. Cloyd went to work to free the old man from the rubble. He worked with the flashlight in his teeth, so he could use both hands. It took time. He fought the panic that was making his head swim. He had to be able to think. What was he going to do? How much time did the old man have? The legs were pinned badly, but at last he freed them, and then he saw the fracture. Surrounded by blood and dirt, the broken bone of the old man's lower leg was sticking out, and it had a sharp point on it.

Cloyd felt dizzy, he felt the panic rising again, and he fought it. He had to get Walter outside. He picked him up as gently as he could and started out of the mine. He didn't know if he'd be strong enough to make it, but he clenched his teeth, straightened his back, and kept moving. Cloyd let the flashlight drop from his fingers as he reached the portal; outside there was moonlight and even the first hint of dawn. Then it came to him, his only chance to get help fast. A helicopter. *A helicopter was coming to get the bear.* He stumbled and then recovered. It felt like he was carrying three hundred pounds. He told himself how light the old man was, and he kept going until he reached the tent.

Cloyd laid Walter down on a sleeping bag, then opened the other bag and spread it across him as a blanket. He knew he had to keep the old man warm. Then he ran down to the creek, drank from it, and splashed his face with the cold water. He had to think, and think right. Rusty said he was going to radio for a helicopter from the guard station. Where was that? He hadn't said—no clues at all. It could be any direction from where he killed the bear. How long would it have taken him to get there? There was no telling. How long before the helicopter came?

Dawn was coming on fast. Rusty probably reached the radio sometime in the evening. The helicopter could be coming anytime now; there was already enough daylight for them to fly. He could take Blueboy and head for the bear and hope to make it in time, but if he didn't—maybe he should ride all the way down the Pine to the trailhead and hitch to a phone and call for a helicopter. He had to choose, and it had to be the right decision. He went back to the old man. Walter was hurt so bad, and he was so fragile. There wasn't time enough to ride all the way down the Pine River, Cloyd decided. There just wasn't enough time.

He left drinking water by the old man's shoulder, in case he came to, and then he saddled the roan. Cloyd walked him to the creek, where he took a long drink, and then a second. "Now we're gonna ride, Blueboy, we're gonna run. I want you to run like you've never run before."

He mounted the horse and took off flying. They galloped down Snowslide Creek and then up the Pine, until they were slowed by the steep Rincon trail. Was there time? Was he doing the right thing?

The roan was climbing, climbing. His gray coat was soaked with sweat, and in the morning light it shone a royal blue. He drank from the Rincon stream when they reached the meadow, and then he broke into a canter when the trail leveled out in the long upper basin. "Atta Blue," Cloyd encouraged him. "Atta Blueboy. Do it for me."

The climb out of the Rincon slowed them to a walk again, and it seemed to take forever. The sun was climbing fast. Noon wasn't that far off. When they were still in the thick mountain willows, he heard the chop-chop-chop of a helicopter and then looked up and saw it for a moment. He waved frantically, but he knew there was no way it could have seen him. At least the copter is heading toward the bear, he thought. It couldn't be on its way out.

The last pitch up the Divide was steep and slow, and the precious minutes were flying by. Finally they topped out. The roan's mouth was all covered with foam, and his sides were heaving. Cloyd urged his horse down the other side. "Run, Blue—it's going to take off! We're not going to make it!"

They came charging off the Divide. The helicopter came in sight, with its whirring blades and the awful noise and commotion they stirred. It was still on the ground. Cloyd couldn't see the bear—it was already loaded. Four men were walking back toward their horses and holding onto their hats. The roan pitched up to a stop and wouldn't budge, not with the chopping and the scent of the bear all around. Cloyd leaped off and ran down the mountainside, and then the men saw him coming. He ran straight for the red-haired man and screamed in his ear. Rusty turned and sprinted, dived low under the whirling blades, and hollered for the pilot to shut the helicopter down.

Six men crowded around him. He told them about the old man, told them to hurry. One of the brothers said, "Hey, how'd you know about this helicopter? How'd you know to come up here?" The red-haired man was watching him closely, and so was the game warden. Cloyd didn't answer. He yelled at them, pleaded for them to hurry. They dragged the bear out of the helicopter. It was enormous.

"You get in with me," the man in uniform said. "You and me and the pilot. Rusty'll take care of your horse."

"Tell Walter," said the outfitter, "tell him I'll bring all of his horses and his stuff out. Tell him not to worry about a thing."

Cloyd looked up and saw the red-haired man's eyes. They were full of concern for his friend; they were even kind for once. The man leaned forward and said, "You done good, boy. However you done it, you done awful good."

Cloyd looked away. He saw the bear all in a heap, with its teeth showing and the tongue caught between them. Flies were buzzing all around, walking in its mouth and on its eyes.

"Let's get moving!" the game warden yelled. He gave Cloyd a push and a boost, then climbed in himself, using the bear for a step.

The copter started up, and then they lifted off. The men and the bear shrank below, and Cloyd caught sight of Blueboy on the mountain. Then they cleared the Divide and headed down the Rincon toward the old man. "So how did you know that helicopter would be coming?" the game warden asked him. "Do you know something about that bear?"

Cloyd knew what Rusty would have told the game warden. Something like what he told his brothers. That the bear charged, and he had to defend himself. He thought about how it really happened. How the bear stood up to sniff the wind, and took the arrow through its neck. He knew this was his chance to get back at the red-haired man, to really show him. His chance to get revenge.

And then Cloyd remembered the peach trees, and his awful revenge with the chain saw. He didn't want any more of that poison. He wouldn't say a thing. What was done was done. Rusty would figure out he'd been right there when it happened—that was enough.

The game warden was waiting for his answer. Cloyd shrugged and looked away, in so final a way that the man could tell he was going to have to wait forever. You might as well wait for a rock to speak.

21

Cloyd wasn't allowed in to see the old man. He came to the hospital every day and waited, but they wouldn't let him in yet. He took the bearstone out of his pocket and asked the nurse to put it by Walter. She said she would put it right on his nightstand where he would see it. Walter's brother was there, from his ranch down at Aztec, and so was his sister-in-law from Missouri. They got to see him first. Finally Cloyd was allowed in. Half of Walter's face was bandaged, and his leg was in a cast that was held off the bed a little with a pulley. He smiled painfully when he saw Cloyd and beckoned him over. "I'm gonna make it, Cloyd," he said. "They can't kill this old hoss."

Cloyd didn't say anything. He didn't know what to

say. He just stood by the old man. Walter rolled his eyes toward the nightstand. "I sure appreciated seeing that blue bear of yours."

Cloyd looked at the bearstone in a new way. He'd been wishing, ever since he'd been to the top of the mountain, that he could find a way to show the old man how he felt about him. Now Cloyd knew what to do. He would give the old man his greatest treasure. "I want you to have it," Cloyd said, pointing to the bearstone with a twist of his lips.

The old man tried to hitch himself up in his bed. "Now wait a minute here, that's—"

Cloyd's eyes met Walter's. He wanted the old man to understand how grateful he was. "I want you to keep it," he said.

Walter saw into Cloyd's dark eyes and felt the strength and conviction of a man, not a boy. He was greatly humbled to receive such a token of affection. And at his age. This was a particular sort of joy he'd never felt in his whole life. He reached over to the nightstand and took the turquoise bear in his fingers. "I'll always treasure this piece, I surely will."

A tear escaped the old man's eye. "I'll think of you every time I see it." For a while Walter couldn't speak. "Now then," he said finally, "you and me have a lot of catchin' up to do. I heard about what you did, how you rode that blue horse up the Divide and got me that helicopter. Nobody else could've done as much, Cloyd."

With a quick smile, Cloyd said, "You would've done the same for me."

And then it was time to go. Walter could only have short visits. It was September, and school was starting. Cloyd came after school to see the old man and talk for a little while, and then the nurses let him come early in the morning as well. Walter was going to be in the hospital a long time. Cloyd could see he really needed company. He told Walter about how school was much better than before, how he was going to learn how to read. His housemother got the school to give him a teacher all to himself for one period a day, since he was going to try.

A few weeks passed, and the old man seemed to be getting worse instead of better. Cloyd didn't know why. He was there when Walter's sister-in-law was saying good-bye, and then he found out something the old man had known for a while, but hadn't told him. "You won't mind it so bad, Walter," she said kindly. "You just can't manage on your own. If I could come and live at the farm, that would be another thing, but you know I have my own family back home. . . ."

"I wouldn't ask you to, Etta," Walter said.

"Well, I know you wouldn't have that. And Tom has his own ranch to keep up with. . . ."

The old man looked away through the window at the yellow leaves blowing from the trees, and he sighed.

His sister-in-law took his hand. "It's time to come in from the farm, Walter. Lots of folks have to face that. The nursing home's not going to be so bad, really, Walter. And I'll know you're getting good care."

The old man reached with his other hand and held fast. "I miss the farm awful bad, Etta. I could get my strength back on the farm."

"The doctor said it's going to be a long, slow process,

Walter. You can't afford a live-in nurse. These bills have drawn you down too bad. Now, we already talked about all that, Walter."

And then she said good-bye. She had to catch a plane back to Missouri. Cloyd sat awhile with the old man. "What's going to happen to the farm?" he asked.

"Have to sell it to pay my board at the nursing home. But now, let's change the subject. Tell me what you did today. . . ."

The reading teacher was talking, and Cloyd wasn't even listening to her. He was thinking about Walter, about how he was getting worse instead of better. Pretty soon they would move him out of the hospital, and then he would wither away. It wouldn't take long. If he couldn't get back to his farm, he was going to wither away.

"Cloyd, I thought you wanted to work with me," the teacher said.

"I'm sorry. I was thinking."

It came to him in the group home, when all the kids were watching television, and he was looking at it but not seeing anything. The next day, in front of the school, Cloyd asked around among the bus drivers and found the one who came in from the east, a burly man in grease-stained overalls. "Does your bus come in from the Piedra?" he asked the driver.

The man shook his head. "Not nearly. Starts this side of Bayfield."

The boy's disappointment showed. "How come you're askin'?" the driver asked.

"I need to come in to school from there."

"Oh? Whereabouts?"

"A farm north of the highway."

"Ain't that the Landis place?"

"You know him?"

"I live out that way. You must be the kid helped out with him in the summer. Hey, I heard about you. Name's Wilson," he said, extending his grimy hand. "Wilson Webb. 'Scuse the grease—I work at a garage in between drivin' the bus. You see, I drive my pickup over to Bayfield and park it where the bus run starts. I'd be happy to bring you in from the Piedra if that's what you're askin'—wouldn't mind the company a bit."

Cloyd hurried back to the group home to tell his housemother. She wasn't there. He went to his room. A boy he'd never met before was unpacking a duffel bag and hanging up his clothes in Cloyd's closet. An army cot was set up between the beds. After a long moment of surprise, Cloyd asked him what was going on.

The boy shrugged. "Heard somebody was moving out. You, I guess."

"I didn't hear anything about it."

Cloyd fretted awhile in the living room, then saw Susan James driving up in the van and hurried out to see her. He stood quietly on the lawn and tried to read her face as she walked up. She knew something important.

"Have I got some news for you, Cloyd," she said excitedly.

Cloyd held his breath. He was always afraid of things dropped on him like this.

"The tribe says you can come home now, Cloyd."

"Home," he mumbled.

"White Mesa! They called this morning, Cloyd, and said everything looks a whole lot better at home, so—"

"How do you mean?" he asked guardedly.

"Well, the tribe heard about how hard you've been trying. They want to give you another chance at going to school right there in Blanding. Your grandmother's new job is working out, and your sister's on her way back from Salt Lake. Maybe your grandmother will get her goats back. Everybody's ready for you to come home, Cloyd."

He didn't know what to say. It was everything he'd hoped for all winter. "When?" he asked blankly.

"Right away! Well, tomorrow morning. Did you meet Charlie—in your room?"

Cloyd nodded.

"Sorry about that. When the people down at Towaoc heard about the vacancy, they sent Charlie up even though they were supposed to wait until tomorrow. But you know, there's a waiting list, and they've been desperately trying to find a place for him. . . . Why don't we go over to the hospital so you can say good-bye to Walter?"

Say good-bye to Walter? How could he do that, he asked himself, when the old man was slipping downhill? If he deserted Walter now. . . As much as he wanted to go back to White Mesa, it wouldn't be right. It was his turn to pay back some of what he'd been given. "I can't go now," he told her. "Maybe after the winter . . ."

"Why not?"

147

"Walter needs me. He can't go back to the farm unless someone's there to do the chores and take care of—"

"But it's all arranged for him to go to the nursing home as soon as he—"

"He'll die there," Cloyd declared. "He's starting to die now."

She knew as much from visiting Walter herself. She'd been worrying terribly for him, knowing how badly he missed his farm. He'd been there so long he was like an old tree too deeply rooted for transplanting. "Tell me how it would all work, Cloyd. I guess you've got it all figured out."

Cloyd told her about the bus driver. He told her she'd have to get permission from the tribe for him to leave the group home and live with Walter.

"And permission from two school districts," she added. "You'd be out of boundaries. I don't know, Cloyd—it all sounds pretty tricky to me. I don't have any idea if the tribe would ever allow something like that. But then again, they might be able to see what kind of sacrifice you'd be making and why. Are you really sure about it yourself?"

Before he could answer, she told him, "Take a long walk and really think it over. Here's your chance to go home, Cloyd. Then come back and let me know what you've decided. If you want to stay with Walter until he's better, I'll do my best to make it happen."

Cloyd walked down to the river to think, crouched on the bank, and turned it all over in his mind. He saw himself standing at the door to a hospital room, discovering the shell of his father hooked up to a machine, and realizing finally that he didn't have a father. He saw himself finding the bearstone and killing the peach trees and following the old man up the Pine River to the mine. He saw himself standing alone atop the Rio Grande Pyramid and realizing a father had come into his life after all. He remembered the look in Blueboy's eye right before he tumbled down the mountain, and he recalled the bear. He'd never forget the bear. . . . *The hurt you get over makes you stronger.* It was all moving in a direction, he decided, making a pattern. And he had to know where it was all leading. If he went home now, he'd never know. It was all part of learning what it meant to live in a good way.

22

It was the second Saturday in November, and they were repairing the foundation under the house. They'd started the weekend before. The project wasn't Walter's idea; Cloyd had remembered him worrying about it during the summer and reminded him of it. Walter had to admit it was a bad situation and getting worse. Walls, roof, and all would start to give before long.

Walter still had the cast on his leg, and he knew he couldn't negotiate the basement stairs. Wrapped up in a blanket, he sat in a chair at the top of the landing, where he could see the boy down below. He had to content himself with lending know-how and moral support.

Cloyd was mixing concrete. He'd carried the hundred-pound bags of cement downstairs himself, as well as countless buckets of sand and gravel, and now he was making concrete. It was chilly in the basement, but as long as he was working, he was warm enough in his denim jacket. He was happy taking care of the old man. He'd grown so used to wandering alone in the canyons, wandering alone in the school corridors, having his own private world. Now he wasn't alone anymore.

Cloyd felt strong. He could do whatever he set his mind to. He was never going to give up—he had a life to live. "Maybe it's all you've got," the old man had said. "Might as well make the most of it."

If he ever had any children, he was going to care about them, the way Walter cared. If he ever had a son, he was going to name him Walter. The old man would be dead and buried by then, he realized. It wouldn't matter. He would show them Walter's picture, and one day he would take them up to the meadows of the Pine River.

Cloyd checked the batch of concrete he was mixing. It was just about right. More water would weaken it. He hoped the weather would give them a few days. The snow from the October storm had thawed, leaving the ground unprotected. With the cold air moving in, he worried that the earth was freezing solid at this very moment. They needed the soil outside that broken wall to have some give in it, so there'd be room for the wall to move over. Cloyd had another reason, too, for hoping the ground would keep a few days and he could dig in it. Thinking about his secret reason made him feel good. He wished for a snowstorm that would blanket the ground and keep it warm. Maybe they'd get one—after breakfast he'd seen a thick layer of high clouds advance from the west and cover the sun. A good storm could be on its way. This time, Walter had said, the snow would stick, and winter would have come to stay.

Cloyd poured his concrete into the holes he had dug in the crawl space. Then he troweled the new footers smooth. The work went well, and he was pleased.

So was the old man. "Tomorrow we'll cut those railroad ties so's they fit between our concrete footers and that good wall. Then we'll build a framework between the two walls and jack it tight. With the railroad ties behind it, you know that good wall ain't gonna give. That other'n's gonna have to move over where it belongs."

Cloyd knew the plan by heart. He was pleased that he understood it so well, pleased that he was learning so many new things. When they jacked the framework tight between the two walls, the bulging one would start to give. Every day when he came home from school, he'd go down in the basement and crank the jack a little more. The crack in the wall would close up. When the wall was straight-up-and-down again, they'd simplify the supports that held it.

It was lunchtime, and it was warm in the kitchen with the cookstove fire going. The old man was fixing sandwiches. Walter made up the grocery lists, and Cloyd did the shopping in town. Every few days he'd go to the store during the lunch break at school. He had some friends this year, and sometimes they went with him. The teachers let him keep the groceries in their lounge; they even had a refrigerator for the fresh things. Walter insisted on doing the cooking. Cloyd thought that was fine. The doctor had said Walter needed to be doing things, only nothing strenuous.

On the kitchen table, with Walter's help, Cloyd struggled at writing a letter to his sister and his grandmother. He told them about Walter, how they'd gone into the mountains, that Walter had been hurt, that he was taking care of Walter until he got stronger. He knew Susan James had made sure they'd heard all those things, but he wanted to tell them himself. "I like the mountains, but I miss the desert," he wrote. "It's getting cold here now. Already it snowed once. I feed the horses in the morning, two bales of hay. Pretty soon I will shovel snow off the pond and chop a hole for them to drink. Blueboy is my favorite. He's strong and smart. When I come home, Walter is going to bring Blueboy, too. He's mine to keep."

For dessert they had doughnuts, the store-bought kind caked with powdered sugar. The old man broke one of his long-standing rules by suggesting they eat them in the parlor, where unavoidably the powdered sugar fell to the carpet. "Blends right in," Walter chuckled. "Reminds me of a joke I'll bet you'd like."

The trace of a smile crossed Cloyd's face. "Oh?" he said, anticipating one of the old man's tall tales.

"This fellow was feeding doughnuts to his horse. Another fellow asks him what for. The first fellow says, 'To find out how many he'd eat before he asked for a cup of coffee.'"

Cloyd flashed a wide smile, and his round face shone like the sun. The old man was holding his breath, his head bobbing up and down, cheeks puffed out, lips drawn tight. Cloyd began to laugh, Walter's breath exploded, and then the old man was laughing too until his ears turned red.

They heard a vehicle pull up outside, and both went to the window to see. A young man was getting out of a white pickup with big red letters on the side.

"Durango Hardware and Nursery," Walter said. "Must be lost." The old man took his jacket from the peg in the mudroom and went outside to see if he could give directions.

The driver had taken off the glove on his right hand to turn the pages of his order book. "Here's your receipt," he said mechanically. He tore out a small yellow page and handed it to the old man. "The seedlings are in the back of the truck."

"Seedlings?" Walter protested.

"All paid for. Twenty-two peach trees. You are Cloyd Atcitty, aren't you?" the young man asked, reaching for his back pocket. "The manager gave me this map."

Cloyd stepped up. "I'm Cloyd Atcitty," he said. "I bought them. It was a surprise," he explained, motioning toward the old man with his lips.

For an instant, Walter's eyes found Cloyd's. The boy was glowing with pleasure.

"I never heard of anybody growing peaches around here," the driver offered skeptically. "Too cold, isn't it?"

"I suppose it is. . . ." Walter admitted, winking at Cloyd. "But we'll sure give it a try."

CONNECTIONS

"Where do your ideas come from?" It is a question writers often hear. Will Hobbs lets us in on the secret—or at least part of it. He explains what got him interested in writing Bearstone *and its sequel,* Beardance. *What kinds of stories might be "denning" in your imagination?*

Denning with the Great Bear
Will Hobbs

I believe there's a part of the human heart that longs for wild places. That part of my heart is filled with the forests, the alpine tundra, and the snow-clad peaks of the Weminuche Wilderness in the San Juan Mountains of southwestern Colorado.

Although *Beardance* is fiction, all of the places in the story are real places. Lake Mary Alice, for example, is one of my favorite hiking destinations. The first time I visited Mary Alice, at the foot of Mount Oso, I witnessed the colossal water, ice, and rockfall described in *Beardance*.

Years before I ever thought of writing *Beardance*, I was gathering the knowledge and experiences that would lead me to this story. In 1973, soon after my wife and I came to live in southwestern Colorado, we found teaching jobs in the little town of Pagosa Springs. I was lucky enough to be able to start a class called "Living in the Southwest." Along with my students I was interviewing local oldtimers, exploring in the library, learning about the human history and the natural history of the San Juans. We learned about the legend of the Lost Mine of the Window and the ways of the old sheepherders, and we learned about our neighbors the Utes who still dance the Bear Dance every spring to help bring the bears out of hibernation.

We learned that grizzlies had been plentiful here during the ten thousand or more years that people lived in the San Juans before the miners and settlers came flooding in during the 1870s. And we learned that now there were no more grizzly bears left in Colorado. The last one had been trapped and then killed by a government trapper in the San Juans near the Rio Grande Pyramid in 1952.

What got me started writing *Bearstone*, my first novel, was the surprising news that a grizzly had been killed in the San Juan Mountains; not far from where we were living, in 1979. The bear was killed by an outfitter who said he didn't realize it was a grizzly. The idea I began my story with was that of a Ute boy meeting the last grizzly in Colorado. This being fiction, I got to make up how it would all happen. The boy became Cloyd, with Walter and Rusty soon joining the story.

After the 1979 incident, the experts once again agreed that the grizzlies were all gone. They were extinct in Colorado. I would never have had the heart to invent the idea for *Beardance* if there hadn't been reason to hope that there might still be some left after all. It was a 1990 sighting of a mother grizzly and three cubs by a rancher on horseback that gave me that hope. In the summers following the sighting, bear biologists tested hair samples and other evidence found in the area, and now believe that these remote mountains of southwestern Colorado may indeed be home to a few surviving grizzlies.

Now I could begin to imagine Cloyd returning to the mountains and meeting the mate and the cubs of the bear that had been killed in *Bearstone*. After reading for months, learning all I could about grizzlies and the traditions of native people all across the continent regarding bears, I began work on the novel. I found myself struggling with my early chapters, trying to get the story to come to life, so I decided to take a break from my desk and hike back up to the Window, that spectacular notch in the Continental Divide which I saw as the geographic focus of the story.

Standing in the Window, I could imagine I saw Cloyd and Walter camping down on East Ute Creek far below. I could almost see the entrance to the lost gold mine on the ridge above the creek. And I could imagine Cloyd with the two grizzly cubs, Brownie and Cocoa, as the snow was starting to fall. I practically ran home, my head bursting with ideas for my story. I poured all of my love of the mountains and of bears into the writing, as well as my deep respect for native traditions.

I found my fingers flying all day and into the night. In writing, as in reading, you're imagining what it's like to be someone else, and I was fully imagining being Cloyd Atcitty, at 11,800 feet with winter coming on, risking his life for those grizzly cubs. I completed the novel in a sort of trance, much like his, in a little less than a month. It was a wonderful experience, and I don't know if one like it will ever come again.

■ ■ ■

Cloyd Atcitty is a "natural"—so close to the natural world around him that he feels, as he says, "a part of it all." In these poems, four writers explore the power of the natural world and our part in it. Would Cloyd agree with them? Do you?

the earth is a living thing
Lucille Clifton

is a black shambling bear
ruffling its wild back and tossing
mountains into the sea

is a black hawk circling
the burying ground circling the bones
picked clean and discarded

is a fish black blind in the belly of water
is a diamond blind in the black belly of coal

is a black and living thing
is a favorite child
of the universe
feel her rolling her hand
in its kinky hair
feel her brushing it clean

Baby Bear Moon
Joseph Bruchac and Jonathan London

Long ago a small child
was lost in the snow.
We thought she had frozen,
but when spring came again,
she was seen with a mother bear
and her small cubs.

She had slept
all through the winter
with them, and from then on
the bears were her family
and her friends.

When we walk by on our snowshoes
we will not bother a bear
or her babies. Instead
we think how those small bears
are like our children.
We let them dream together.

Here on This Mountain
Nancy Wood

Here on this mountain I am not alone
For all the lives I used to be are with me.
> I am the Last Great Warrior looking back
> At the white man beating paths
> Up our old game trails.
> I am the Last Young Brave chasing buffalo
> Putting his arrows away.
> I am the Last Young Maiden digging roots
> Leaving her reflection in the water.
> I am the Last Old Woman grinding corn
> Shedding her tears on the earth.
> I am the Last Great Chief standing tall
> Giving thanks for all our great hunts.
> I am the Buffalo, our Brother, and
> The Red-winged Blackbird, our Sister,
> Who have come to say good-by.
> I am the Rocks, the Trees, the River
> Who tell us not to cry.
> I go down the mountain with my people
> Taking away with us
> All we have left behind.
Here on this mountain I am not alone
For all the lives I used to be are with me.
All the lives tell me now I have come home.

■ ■ ■

Clarissa is ". . . a real loner. Not trusting anybody." That also sounds like Cloyd, early in Bearstone. How is Clarissa a "lone bear"? Will she find her place in the world, as Cloyd does? Have you ever felt as she does?

Dancer
Vickie Sears

Tell you just how it was with her. Took her to a dance not long after she come to live with us. Smartest thing I ever done. Seems like some old Eaglespirit woman saw her living down here and came back just to be with Clarissa.

Five years old she was when she come to us. Some foster kids come with lots of stuff, but she came with everything she had in a paper bag. Some dresses that was too short. A pair of pants barely holding a crotch. A pile of ratty underwear and one new nightgown. Mine was her third foster home in as many months. The agency folks said she was *so-cio-path-ic.* I don't know nothing from that. She just seemed like she was all full up with anger and scaredness like lots of the kids who come to me. Only she was a real loner. Not trusting nobody. But she ran just like any other kid, was quiet when needed. Smiled at all the right times. If you could get her to smile, that is. Didn't talk much, though.

Had these ferocious dreams, too. Real screamer dreams they were. Shake the soul right out of you. She'd be screaming and crying with her little body wriggling on the bed, her hair all matted up on her woody-colored face. One time I got her to tell me what she was seeing, and she told me how she was being chased by a man with a long knife what he was going to kill her with and nobody could hear her calling out for help. She didn't talk too much about them, but they was all bad like that one. Seemed the most fierce dreams I ever remember anybody ever having outside of a vision seek. They said her tribe was Assiniboin, but they weren't for certain. What was for sure was that she was a fine dark-eyed girl just meant for someone to scoop up for loving.

Took her to her first dance in September, like I said, not long after she came. It wasn't like I thought it would be a good thing to do. It was just that we was all going. Me, my own kids, some nieces and nephews and the other children who was living with us. The powwow was just part of what we done all the time. Every month. More often in the summer. But this was the regular first Friday night of the school year. We'd all gather up and go to the school. I was thinking on leaving her home with a sitter cause she'd tried to kill one of the cats a couple of days before. We'd had us a big talk and she was grounded, but, well, it seemed like she ought to be with us.

Harold, that's my oldest boy, he and the other kids was mad with her, but he decided to show her around anyhow. At the school he went through the gym telling people, "This here's my sister, Clarissa." Wasn't no fuss or anything. She was just another one of the kids. When they was done meeting folks, he put her on one of the bleachers near the drum and went to join the men. He was in that place where his voice cracks but was real proud to be drumming. Held his hand up to his ear even, some of the time. Anyhow, Clarissa was sitting there, not all that inter-ested in the dance or drum, when Molly Graybull come out in her button dress. Her arms was all stretched out, and she was slipping around, preening on them spindles of legs that get skin-nier with every year. She was well into her seventies, and I might as well admit, Molly had won herself a fair share of dance con-tests. So it wasn't no surprise how a little girl could get so fixated on Molly. Clarissa watched her move around-around-around.

Then all the rest of the dancers after Molly. She sure took in a good eyeful. Fancy dance. Owl dance. Circle dance. Even a hoop dancer was visiting that night. Everything weaving all slow, then fast. Around-around until that child couldn't see nothing else. Seemed like she was struck silent in the night, too. Never had no dreams at all. Well, not the hollering kind anyways.

Next day she was more quiet than usual only I could see she was looking at her picture book and tapping the old one-two, one-two. Tapping her toes on the rug with the inside of her head going around and around. As quiet as she could be, she was.

A few days went on before she asks me, "When's there gonna be another dance?"

I tell her in three weeks. She just smiles and goes on outside, waiting on the older kids to come home from school.

The very next day she asks if she can listen to some singing. I give her the tape recorder and some of Joe Washington from up to the Lummi reservation and the Kicking Woman Singers. Clarissa, she takes them tapes and runs out back behind the chicken shed, staying out all afternoon. I wasn't worried none, though, cause I could hear the music the whole time. Matter of fact, it like to make me sick of them same songs come the end of three weeks. But that kid, she didn't get into no kind of mischief. Almost abnormal how good she was. Worried me some to see her so caught up but it seemed good too. The angry part of her slowed down so's she wasn't hitting the animals or chopping on herself with sticks like she was doing when she first come. She wasn't laughing much either, but she started playing with the other kids when they come home. Seemed like everybody was working hard to be better with each other.

Come March, Clarissa asks, "Can I dance?"

For sure, the best time for teaching is when a kid wants to listen, so we stood side to side with me doing some steps. She followed along fine. I put on a tape and started moving faster, and

Clarissa just kept up all natural. I could tell she'd been practicing lots. She was doing real good.

Comes the next powwow, which was outside on the track field, I braided Clarissa's hair. Did her up with some ermine and bead ties, then give her a purse to carry. It was all beaded with a rose and leaves. Used to be my aunt's. She held it right next to her side with her chin real high. She joined in a Circle dance. I could see she was watching her feet a little and looking how others do their steps, but mostly she was doing wonderful. When Molly Graybull showed up beside her, Clarissa took to a seat and stared. She didn't dance again that night, but I could see there was dreaming coming into her eyes. I saw that fire that said to practice. And she did. I heard her every day in her room. Finally bought her her very own tape recorder so's the rest of us could listen to music too.

Some months passed on. All the kids was getting bigger. Clarissa, she went into the first grade. Harvey went off to community college up in Seattle, and that left me with Ronnie being the oldest at home. Clarissa was keeping herself busy all the time going over to Molly Graybull's. She was coming home with Spider Woman stories and trickster tales. One night she speaks up at supper and says, right clear and loud, "I'm an Assiniboin." Clear as it can be, she says it again. Don't nobody have to say nothing to something that proud said.

Next day I started working on a wing dress for Clarissa. She was going to be needing one for sure real soon.

Comes the first school year powwow and everyone was putting on their best. I called for Clarissa to come to my room. I told her, "I think it's time you have something special for yourself." Then I held up the green satin and saw her eyes full up with glitter. She didn't say nothing. Only kisses me and runs off to her room.

Just as we're all getting out of the car, Clarissa whispered to me, "I'm gonna dance with Molly Graybull." I put my hand on her shoulder to say, "You just listen to your spirit. That's where your music is."

We all danced an Owl dance, a Friendship dance, and a couple of Circle dances. Things was feeling real warm and good, and then it was time for the women's traditional. Clarissa joined the circle. She opened her arms to something nobody but her seemed to hear. That's when I saw that old Eagle woman come down and slide right inside of Clarissa, scooping up that child. There Clarissa was, full up with music. All full with that old, old spirit, letting herself dance through Clarissa's feet. Then Molly Graybull come dancing alongside Clarissa, and they was both the same age.

■ ■ ■

Not all lessons come from a classroom or a textbook. In Bearstone, *Cloyd learns about himself by experiencing the natural world of the Southwest. In these two poems, Pat Mora shares some lessons that came to her in similar experiences. What can you learn from her?*

Lesson 1
Pat Mora

The desert is powerless
when thunder shakes the hot air
and unfamiliar raindrops slide
on rocks, sand, *mesquite,*
when unfamiliar raindrops overwhelm
her, distort her face.
But after the storm, she breathes deeply,
caressed by a fresh sweet calm.
My Mother smiles rainbows.

When I feel shaken, powerless
to stop my bruising sadness,
I hear My Mother whisper:

Mi'ja

don't fear your hot tears
cry away the storm, then listen, listen.

Lesson 2
Pat Mora

Small, white fairies dance
on the *Rio Grande*. Usually they swim
deep through their days and nights
hiding from our eyes, but when the white
sun pulls them up, up
they leap about, tiny shimmering stars.

The desert says: feel the sun
luring you from your dark, sad waters,
burst through the surface
                              dance

■ ■ ■

*Cloyd picks Blueboy and Kennie chooses Flicka. Stories about the
bond between people and horses have been favorites for as long as
people have ridden horses. Among these stories, "My Friend Flicka"
is a classic.*

My Friend Flicka
Mary O'Hara

*Kennie never seemed to do anything right. "If I could have a
colt all for my own," he said, "I might do better."*

Report cards for the second semester were sent out soon after
school closed in mid-June.

Kennie's was a shock to the whole family.

"If I could have a colt all for my own," said Kennie, "I might
do better."

Rob McLaughlin glared at his son. "Just as a matter of
curiosity," he said, "how do you go about it to get a zero in an
examination? Forty in arithmetic; seventeen in history! But a
zero? Just as one man to another, what goes on in your head?"

"Yes, tell us how you do it, Ken," chirped Howard.

"Eat your breakfast, Howard," snapped his mother.

Kennie's blond head bent over his plate until his face was
almost hidden. His cheeks burned.

McLaughlin finished his coffee and pushed his chair back.
"You'll do an hour a day on your lessons all through the
summer."

Nell McLaughlin saw Kennie wince as if something had
actually hurt him.

Lessons and study in the summertime, when the long winter was just over and there weren't hours enough in the day for

all the things he wanted to do!

Kennie took things hard. His eyes turned to the wide-open window with a look almost of despair.

The hill opposite the house, covered with arrow-straight jack pines, was sharply etched in the thin air of the eight-thousand-foot altitude. Where it fell away, vivid green grass ran up to meet it; and over range and upland poured the strong Wyoming sunlight that stung everything into burning color. A big jack rabbit sat under one of the pines, waving his long ears back and forth.

Ken had to look at his plate and blink back tears before he could turn to his father and say carelessly, "Can I help you in the corral with the horses this morning, Dad?"

"You'll do your study every morning before you do any-thing else." And McLaughlin's scarred boots and heavy spurs clattered across the kitchen floor. "I'm disgusted with you. Come, Howard."

Howard strode after his father, nobly refraining from looking at Kennie.

"Help me with the dishes, Kennie," said Nell McLaughlin as she rose, tied on a big apron, and began to clear the table.

Kennie looked at her in despair. She poured steaming water into the dishpan and sent him for the soap powder.

"If I could have a colt," he muttered again.

"Now get busy with that dish towel, Ken. It's eight o'clock. You can study till nine and then go up to the corral. They'll still be there."

At supper that night, Kennie said, "But Dad, Howard had a colt all of his own when he was only eight. And he trained it and schooled it all himself; and now he's eleven and Highboy is three, and he's riding him. I'm nine now, and even if you did give me a colt now, I couldn't catch up to Howard because I couldn't ride it till it was a three-year-old and then I'd be twelve."

Nell laughed, "Nothing wrong with that arithmetic."

But Rob said, "Howard never gets less than seventy-five average at school, and hasn't disgraced himself and his family by getting more demerits than any other boy in his class."

Kennie didn't answer. He couldn't figure it out. He tried hard; he spent hours poring over his books. That was supposed to get you good marks, but it never did. Everyone said he was bright; why was it that when he studied he didn't learn? He had a vague feeling that perhaps he looked out the window too much, or looked through the walls to see clouds and sky and hills and wonder what was happening out there. Sometimes it wasn't even a wonder but just a pleasant drifting feeling of nothing at all, as if nothing mattered, as if there was always plenty of time, as if the lessons would get done of themselves. And then the bell would ring and study period was over.

If he had a colt . . .

When the boys had gone to bed that night, Nell McLaughlin sat down with her overflowing mending basket and glanced at her husband.

He was at his desk as usual, working on account books and inventories.

Nell threaded a darning needle and thought, "It's either that whacking big bill from the vet for the mare that died or the last half of the tax bill."

It didn't seem just the auspicious moment to plead Kennie's cause. But then, these days, there was always a line between Rob's eyes and a harsh note in his voice.

"Rob," she began.

He flung down his pencil and turned around.

"That law!" he exclaimed.

"What law?"

"The state law that puts high taxes on pedigreed stock. I'll have to do as the rest of 'em do—drop the papers."

"Drop the papers! But you'll never get decent prices if you don't have registered horses."

"I don't get decent prices now."

"But you will someday, if you don't drop the papers."

"Maybe." He bent again over the desk.

Rob, thought Nell, was a lot like Kennie himself. He set his heart. Oh, how stubbornly he set his heart on just some one thing he wanted above everything else. He had set his heart on horses and ranching way back when he had been a crack rider at West Point; and he had resigned and thrown away his army career just for the horses. Well, he'd got what he wanted.

She drew a deep breath, snipped her thread, laid down the sock, and again looked across at her husband as she unrolled another length of darning cotton.

To get what you want is one thing, she was thinking. The three-thousand-acre ranch and the hundred head of horses. But to make it pay—for a dozen or more years they had been trying to make it pay. People said ranching hadn't paid since the beef barons ran their herds on public land; people said the only prosperous ranchers in Wyoming were the dude ranchers; people said . . .

But suddenly she gave her head a little rebellious, gallant shake. Rob would always be fighting and struggling against something, like Kennie, perhaps like herself too. Even those first years when there was no water piped into the house, when every day brought a new difficulty or danger, how she had loved it! How she still loved it!

She ran the darning ball into the toe of a sock, Kennie's sock. The length of it gave her a shock. Yes, the boys were growing up fast, and now Kennie—Kennie and the colt . . .

After a while she said, "Give Kennie a colt, Rob."

"He doesn't deserve it." The answer was short. Rob pushed away his papers and took out his pipe.

"Howard's too far ahead of him; older and bigger and quicker and his wits about him, and . . ."

"Ken doesn't half try, doesn't stick at anything."

She put down her sewing. "He's crazy for a colt of his own. He hasn't had another idea in his head since you gave Highboy to Howard."

"I don't believe in bribing children to do their duty."

"Not a bribe." She hesitated.

"No? What would you call it?"

She tried to think it out. "I just have a feeling Ken isn't going to pull anything off, and"—her eyes sought Rob's—"it's time he did. It isn't the school marks alone, but I just don't want things to go on any longer with Ken never coming out at the right end of anything."

"I'm beginning to think he's just dumb."

"He's not dumb. Maybe a little thing like this—if he had a colt of his own, trained him, rode him . . ."

Rob interrupted. "But it isn't a little thing, nor an easy thing, to break and school a colt the way Howard has schooled Highboy. I'm not going to have a good horse spoiled by Ken's careless ways. He goes woolgathering. He never knows what he's doing."

"But he'd *love* a colt of his own, Rob. If he could do it, it might make a big difference in him."

"*If* he could do it! But that's a big if."

At breakfast next morning, Kennie's father said to him, "When you've done your study, come out to the barn. I'm going in the car up to section twenty-one this morning to look over the brood mares.[1] You can go with me."

"Can I go too, Dad?" cried Howard.

McLaughlin frowned at Howard. "You turned Highboy out

---

1 **brood mares:** female horses kept for breeding.

last evening with dirty legs."

Howard wriggled. "I groomed him. . . ."

"Yes, down to his knees."

"He kicks."

"And whose fault is that? You don't get on his back again until I see his legs clean."

The two boys eyed each other, Kennie secretly triumphant and Howard chagrined.[2] McLaughlin turned at the door, "And, Ken, a week from today I'll give you a colt. Between now and then you can decide what one you want."

Kennie shot out of his chair and stared at his father. "A—a—spring colt, Dad, or a yearling?"

McLaughlin was somewhat taken aback, but his wife concealed a smile. If Kennie got a yearling colt, he would be even up with Howard.

"A yearling colt, your father means, Ken," she said smoothly. "Now hurry with your lessons. Howard will wipe."

Kennie found himself the most important personage on the ranch. Prestige lifted his head, gave him an inch more of height and a bold stare, and made him feel different all the way through. Even Gus and Tim Murphy, the ranch hands, were more interested in Kennie's choice of a colt than anything else.

Howard was fidgety with suspense. "Who'll you pick, Ken? Say—pick Doughboy, why don't you? Then when he grows up, he'll be sort of twins with mine, in his name anyway. Doughboy, Highboy, see?"

The boys were sitting on the worn wooden step of the door which led from the tack room into the corral, busy with rags and polish, shining their bridles.

Ken looked at his brother with scorn. Doughboy would never have half of Highboy's speed.

"Lassie, then," suggested Howard. "She's black as ink, like

2 **chagrined** (shə·grĭnd´): embarrassed.

mine. And she'll be fast. . . ."

"Dad says Lassie'll never go over fifteen hands."[3]

Nell McLaughlin saw the change in Kennie and her hopes rose. He went to his books in the morning with determination and really studied. A new alertness took the place of the day-dreaming. Examples in arithmetic were neatly written out, and, as she passed his door before breakfast, she often heard the monot-onous drone of his voice as he read his American history aloud.

Each night, when he kissed her, he flung his arms around her and held her fiercely for a moment, then, with a winsome and blissful smile into her eyes, turned away to bed.

He spent days inspecting the different bands of horses and colts. He sat for hours on the corral fence, very important, chewing straws. He rode off on one of the ponies for half the day, wandering through the mile-square pastures that ran down toward the Colorado border.

And when the week was up, he announced his decision. "I'll take that yearling filly of Rocket's. The sorrel[4] with the cream tail and mane."

His father looked at him in surprise. "The one that got tangled in the barbed wire?—that's never been named?"

In a second all Kennie's new pride was gone. He hung his head defensively. "Yes."

"You've made a bad choice, Son. You couldn't have picked a worse."

"She's fast, Dad. And Rocket's fast. . . ."

"It's the worst line of horses I've got. There's never one among them with real sense. The mares are hellions[5] and the stallions outlaws; they're untamable."

"I'll tame her."

---

3 **fifteen hands:** 60 inches (about 150 centimeters) in height.

4 **sorrel:** a horse of reddish brown color.

5 **hellions:** troublemakers.

Rob guffawed. "Not I, nor anyone, has ever really been able to tame any one of them."

Kennie's chest heaved.

"Better change your mind, Ken. You want a horse that'll be a real friend to you, don't you?"

"Yes"—Kennie's voice was unsteady.

"Well, you'll never make a friend of that filly. She's all cut and scarred up already with tearing through barbed wire after that no-good mother of hers. No fence'll hold 'em. . . ."

"I know," said Kennie, still more faintly.

"Change your mind?" asked Howard briskly.

"No."

Rob was grim and put out. He couldn't go back on his word. The boy had to have a reasonable amount of help in breaking and taming the filly, and he could envision precious hours, whole days, wasted in the struggle.

Nell McLaughlin despaired. Once again Ken seemed to have taken the wrong turn and was back where he had begun, stoical, silent, defensive.

But there was a difference that only Ken could know. The way he felt about his colt. The way his heart sang. The pride and joy that filled him so full that sometimes he hung his head so they wouldn't see it shining out of his eyes.

He had known from the very first that he would choose that particular yearling because he was in love with her.

The year before, he had been out working with Gus, the big Swedish ranch hand, on the irrigation ditch, when they had noticed Rocket standing in a gully on the hillside, quiet for once and eyeing them cautiously.

"Ay bet she got a colt," said Gus, and they walked carefully up the draw.[6] Rocket gave a wild snort, thrust her feet out, shook her head wickedly, then fled away. And as they reached

---

6 **draw:** gully.

the spot, they saw standing there the wavering, pinkish colt, barely able to keep its feet. It gave a little squeak and started after its mother on crooked, wobbling legs.

"Yee whiz! Luk at de little flicka!" said Gus.

"What does flicka mean, Gus?"

"Swedish for 'little gurl,' Ken. . . ."

Ken announced at supper, "You said she'd never been named. I've named her. Her name is Flicka."

The first thing to do was to get her in. She was running with a band of yearlings on the saddleback,[7] cut with ravines and gullies, on section twenty.

They all went out after her, Ken, as owner, on old Rob Roy, the wisest horse on the ranch.

Ken was entranced to watch Flicka when the wild band of youngsters discovered that they were being pursued and took off across the mountain. Footing made no difference to her. She floated across the ravines, always two lengths ahead of the others. Her pink mane and tail whipped in the wind. Her long, delicate legs had only to aim, it seemed, at a particular spot for her to reach it and sail on. She seemed to Ken a fairy horse.

He sat motionless, just watching and holding Rob Roy in, when his father thundered past on Sultan and shouted, "Well, what's the matter? Why didn't you turn 'em?"

Kennie woke up and galloped after.

Rob Roy brought in the whole band. The corral gates were closed, and an hour was spent shunting the ponies in and out through the chutes, until Flicka was left alone in the small round corral in which the baby colts were branded. Gus drove the others away, out of the gate, and up the saddleback.

But Flicka did not intend to be left. She hurled herself against the poles which walled the corral. She tried to jump them. They

---

7 **saddleback:** a hill or ridge with a depression at the top, like the back of a horse that has worn a saddle too long.

were seven feet high. She caught her front feet over the top rung, clung, scrambled, while Kennie held his breath for fear the slender legs would be caught between the bars and snapped. Her hold broke; she fell over backward, rolled, screamed, tore around the corral. Kennie had a sick feeling in the pit of his stomach, and his father looked disgusted.

One of the bars broke. She hurled herself again. Another went. She saw the opening and, as neatly as a dog crawls through a fence, inserted her head and forefeet, scrambled through, and fled away, bleeding in a dozen places.

As Gus was coming back, just about to close the gate to the upper range, the sorrel whipped through it, sailed across the road and ditch with her inimitable floating leap, and went up the side of the saddleback like a jack rabbit.

From way up the mountain, Gus heard excited whinnies, as she joined the band he had just driven up, and the last he saw of them they were strung out along the crest running like deer.

"Yee whiz!" said Gus, and stood motionless and staring until the ponies had disappeared over the ridge. Then he closed the gate, remounted Rob Roy, and rode back to the corral.

Rob McLaughlin gave Kennie one more chance to change his mind. "Last chance, Son. Better pick a horse that you have some hope of riding one day. I'd have got rid of this whole line of stock if they weren't so fast that I've had the fool idea that some day there might turn out one gentle one in the lot—and I'd have a racehorse. But there's never been one so far, and it's not going to be Flicka."

"It's not going to be Flicka," chanted Howard.

"Perhaps she *might* be gentled," said Kennie; and Nell, watching, saw that although his lips quivered, there was fanatical determination in his eye.

"Ken," said Rob, "it's up to you. If you say you want her, we'll get her. But she wouldn't be the first of that line to die rather than give in. They're beautiful and they're fast, but let me tell you this, young man, they're *loco!*"[8]

Kennie flinched under his father's direct glance.

"If I go after her again, I'll not give up whatever comes, understand what I mean by that?"

"Yes."

"What do you say?"

"I want her."

They brought her in again. They had better luck this time. She jumped over the Dutch half door of the stable and crashed inside. The men slammed the upper half of the door shut and she was caught.

The rest of the band were driven away, and Kennie stood outside the stable, listening to the wild hoofs beating, the screams, the crashes. His Flicka inside there! He was drenched with perspiration.

"We'll leave her to think it over," said Rob when dinnertime came. "Afterward, we'll go up and feed and water her."

But when they went up afterward there was no Flicka in the barn. One of the windows, higher than the mangers, was broken.

The window opened into a pasture an eighth of a mile square, fenced in barbed wire six feet high. Near the stable stood a wagonload of hay. When they went around the back of the stable to see where Flicka had hidden herself, they found her between the stable and the hay wagon, eating.

At their approach she leaped away, then headed east across the pasture.

"If she's like her mother," said Rob, "she'll go right through the wire."

"Ay bet she'll go over," said Gus. "She yumps like a deer."

"No horse can jump that," said McLaughlin.

---

8 *loco:* the Spanish word for "crazy."

Kennie said nothing because he could not speak. It was, perhaps, the most terrible moment of his life. He watched Flicka racing toward the eastern wire.

A few yards from it, she swerved, turned, and raced diagonally south.

"It turned her! It turned her!" cried Kennie, almost sobbing. It was the first sign of hope for Flicka. "Oh, Dad! She has got sense. She has! She has!"

Flicka turned again as she met the southern boundary of the pasture; again at the northern; she avoided the barn. Without abating anything of her whirlwind speed, following a precise, accurate calculation and turning each time on a dime, she investigated every possibility. Then, seeing that there was no hope, she raced south toward the range where she had spent her life, gathered herself, and shot into the air.

Each of the three men watching had the impulse to cover his eyes, and Kennie gave a sort of howl of despair.

Twenty yards of fence came down with her as she hurled herself through. Caught on the upper strands, she turned a complete somersault, landing on her back, her four legs dragging the wire down on top of her, and tangling herself in them beyond hope of escape.

"Blasted wire!" said McLaughlin. "If I could afford decent fences . . ."

Kennie followed the men miserably as they walked to the filly. They stood in a circle, watching while she kicked and fought and thrashed until the wire was tightly wound and knotted about her, cutting, piercing, and tearing great three-cornered pieces of flesh and hide. At last she was unconscious, streams of blood running on her golden coat, and pools of crimson widening and spreading on the grass beneath her.

With the wire cutter which Gus always carried in the hip pocket of his overalls, he cut all the wire away, and they drew her into the pasture, repaired the fence, placed hay, a box of oats, and a tub of water near her, and called it a day.

"I don't think she'll pull out of it," said McLaughlin.

Next morning Kennie was up at five, doing his lessons. At six he went out to Flicka.

She had not moved. Food and water were untouched. She was no longer bleeding, but the wounds were swollen and caked over.

Kennie got a bucket of fresh water and poured it over her mouth. Then he leaped away, for Flicka came to life, scrambled up, got her balance, and stood swaying.

Kennie went a few feet away and sat down to watch her. When he went into breakfast, she had drunk deeply of the water and was mouthing the oats.

There began, then, a sort of recovery. She ate, drank, limped about the pasture; stood for hours with hanging head and weakly splayed-out[9] legs, under the clump of cottonwood trees. The swollen wounds scabbed and began to heal.

Kennie lived in the pasture, too. He followed her around; he talked to her. He too lay snoozing or sat under the cotton-woods; and often, coaxing her with hand outstretched, he walked very quietly toward her. But she would not let him come near her.

Often she stood with her head at the south fence, looking off to the mountain. It made the tears come to Kennie's eyes to see the way she longed to get away.

Still Rob said she wouldn't pull out of it. There was no use putting a halter on her. She had no strength.

One morning, as Ken came out of the house, Gus met him and said, "De filly's down."

Kennie ran to the pasture, Howard close behind him. The

---

9 **splayed-out:** spread outward.

right hind leg, which had been badly swollen at the knee joint, had opened in a festering wound, and Flicka lay flat and motionless, with staring eyes.

"Don't you wish now you'd chosen Doughboy?" asked Howard.

"Go away!" shouted Ken.

Howard stood watching while Kennie sat down on the ground and took Flicka's head on his lap. Though she was conscious and moved a little, she did not struggle or seem frightened. Tears rolled down Kennie's cheeks as he talked to her and petted her. After a few moments, Howard walked away.

"Mother, what do you do for an infection when it's a horse?" asked Kennie.

"Just what you'd do if it was a person. Wet dressings. I'll help you, Ken. We mustn't let those wounds close or scab over until they're clean. I'll make a poultice[10] for that hind leg and help you put it on. Now that she'll let us get close to her, we can help her a lot."

"The thing to do is see that she eats," said Rob. "Keep up her strength."

But he himself would not go near her. "She won't pull out of it," he said. "I don't want to see her or think about her."

Kennie and his mother nursed the filly. The big poultice was bandaged on the hind leg. It drew out much poisoned matter, and Flicka felt better and was able to stand again.

She watched for Kennie now and followed him like a dog, hopping on three legs, holding up the right hind leg with its huge knob of a bandage in comical fashion.

"Dad, Flicka's my friend now; she likes me," said Ken.

His father looked at him. "I'm glad of that, Son. It's a fine

---

10 **poultice** (pōl´tis): a warm, moist dressing for a wound.

thing to have a horse for a friend."

Kennie found a nicer place for her. In the lower pasture the brook ran over cool stones. There was a grassy bank, the size of a corral, almost on a level with the water. Here she could lie softly, eat grass, drink fresh running water. From the grass, a twenty-foot hill sloped up, crested with overhanging trees. She was enclosed, as it were, in a green, open-air nursery.

Kennie carried her oats, morning and evening. She would watch for him to come, eyes and ears pointed to the hill. And one evening, Ken, still some distance off, came to a stop and a wide grin spread over his face. He had heard her nicker.[11] She had caught sight of him coming and was calling to him!

He placed the box of oats under her nose, and she ate while he stood beside her, his hand smoothing the satin-soft skin under her mane. It had a nap as deep as plush. He played with her long, cream-colored tresses, arranged her forelock neatly between her eyes. She was a bit dish-faced, like an Arab, with eyes set far apart. He lightly groomed and brushed her while she stood turning her head to him whichever way he went.

He spoiled her. Soon she would not step to the stream to drink but he must hold a bucket for her. And she would drink, then lift her dripping muzzle, rest it on the shoulder of his blue chambray shirt, her golden eyes dreaming off into the distance, then daintily dip her mouth to drink again.

When she turned her head to the south and pricked her ears and stood tense and listening, Ken knew she heard the other colts galloping on the upland.

"You'll go back there someday, Flicka, he whispered. "You'll be three and I'll be eleven. You'll be so strong you won't know I'm on your back, and we'll fly like the wind. We'll stand on the very top where we can look over the whole world and smell the snow from the Never-Summer Range. Maybe

---

11 **nicker:** whinny.

we'll see antelope. . . ."

This was the happiest month of Kennie's life.

With the morning, Flicka always had new strength and would hop three-legged up the hill to stand broadside to the early sun, as horses love to do.

The moment Ken woke, he'd go to the window and see her there; and when he was dressed and at his table studying, he sat so that he could raise his head and see Flicka.

After breakfast, she would be waiting for him and the box of oats at the gate, and for Nell McLaughlin with fresh bandages and buckets of disinfectant; and all three would go together to the brook, Flicka hopping along ahead of them, as if she were leading the way.

But Rob McLaughlin would not look at her.

One day all the wounds were swollen again. Presently they opened, one by one; and Kennie and his mother made more poultices.

Still the little filly climbed the hill in the early morning and ran about on three legs. Then she began to go down in flesh and almost overnight wasted away to nothing. Every rib showed; the glossy hide was dull and brittle, and was pulled over the skeleton as if she were a dead horse.

Gus said, "It's de fever. It burns up her flesh. If you could stop de fever she might get vell."

McLaughlin was standing in his window one morning and saw the little skeleton hopping about three-legged in the sunshine, and he said, "That's the end. I won't have a thing like that on my place."

Kennie had to understand that Flicka had not been getting well all this time; she had been slowly dying.

"She still eats her oats," he said mechanically.

They were all sorry for Ken. Nell McLaughlin stopped disinfecting and dressing the wounds. "It's no use Ken," she said gently. "You know Flicka's going to die, don't you?"

"Yes, Mother."

Ken stopped eating. Howard said, "Ken doesn't eat anything any more. Don't he have to eat his dinner, Mother?"

But Nell answered, "Leave him alone."

Because the shooting of wounded animals is all in the day's work on the Western plains, and sickening to everyone, Rob's voice, when he gave the order to have Flicka shot, was as flat as if he had been telling Gus to kill a chicken for dinner.

"Here's the Marlin, Gus. Pick out a time when Ken's not around and put the filly out of her misery."

Gus took the rifle. "*Ja*, Boss. . . ."

Ever since Ken had known that Flicka was to be shot, he had kept his eye on the rack which held the firearms. His father allowed no firearms in the bunkhouse. The gun rack was in the dining room of the ranch house; and, going through it to the kitchen three times a day for meals, Ken's eye scanned the weapons to make sure that they were all there.

That night they were not all there. The Marlin rifle was missing.

When Kennie saw that, he stopped walking. He felt dizzy. He kept staring at the gun rack, telling himself that it surely was there—he counted again and again—he couldn't see clearly. . . .

Then he felt an arm across his shoulder and heard his father's voice.

"I know, Son. Some things are awful hard to take. We just have to take 'em. I have to, too."

Kennie got hold of his father's hand and held on. It helped steady him.

Finally he looked up. Rob looked down and smiled at him and gave him a little shake and squeeze. Ken managed a smile too.

"All right now?"

"All right, Dad."

They walked in to supper together.

Ken even ate a little. But Nell looked thoughtfully at the ashen color of his face, and at the little pulse that was beating in the side of his neck.

After supper he carried Flicka her oats, but he had to coax her and she would only eat a little. She stood with her head hanging, but when he stroked it and talked to her, she pressed her face into his chest and was content. He could feel the burning heat of her body. It didn't seem possible that anything so thin could be alive.

Presently Kennie saw Gus come into the pasture, carrying the Marlin. When he saw Ken, he changed his direction and sauntered along as if he were out to shoot some cottontails.

Ken ran to him. "When are you going to do it, Gus?"

"Ay was goin' down soon now, before it got dark. . . ."

"Gus, don't do it tonight. Wait till morning. Just one more night, Gus."

"Vell, in de morning, den, but it got to be done, Ken. Yer fader gives de order."

"I know. I won't say anything more."

An hour after the family had gone to bed, Ken got up and put on his clothes. It was a warm moonlit night. He ran down to the brook, calling softly, "Flicka! Flicka!"

But Flicka did not answer with a little nicker, and she was not in the nursery nor hopping about the pasture. Ken hunted for an hour.

At last he found her down the creek, lying in the water. Her head had been on the bank, but as she lay there, the current of the stream had sucked and pulled at her, and she had had no strength to resist; and little by little her head had slipped down until when Ken got there only the muzzle was resting on the bank, and the body and legs were swinging in the stream.

Kennie slid into the water, sitting on the bank, and he

hauled at her head. But she was heavy, and the current dragged like a weight; and he began to sob because he had no strength to draw her out.

Then he found a leverage for his heels against some rocks in the bed of the stream, and he braced himself against these and pulled with all his might; and her head came up onto his knees, and he held it cradled in his arms.

He was glad that she had died of her own accord, in the cool water, under the moon, instead of being shot by Gus. Then, putting his face close to hers and looking searchingly into her eyes, he saw that she was alive and looking back at him.

And then he burst out crying and hugged her and said, "Oh, my little Flicka, my little Flicka."

The long night passed.

The moon slid slowly across the heavens.

The water rippled over Kennie's legs and over Flicka's body. And gradually the heat and fever went out of her. And the cool running water washed and washed her wounds.

When Gus went down in the morning with the rifle, they hadn't moved. There they were, Kennie sitting in water over his thighs and hips, with Flicka's head in his arms.

Gus seized Flicka by the head and hauled her out on the grassy bank, and then, seeing that Kennie couldn't move, cold and stiff and half paralyzed as he was, lifted him in his arms and carried him to the house.

"Gus," said Ken through chattering teeth, "don't shoot her, Gus."

"It ain't fur me to say, Ken. You know dat."

"But the fever's left her, Gus."

"Ay wait a little, Ken. . . ."

Rob McLaughlin drove to Laramie to get the doctor, for Ken was in violent chills that would not stop. His mother had him in bed, wrapped in hot blankets, when they got back.

He looked at his father imploringly as the doctor shook down the thermometer.

"She might get well now, Dad. The fever's left her. It went out of her when the moon went down."

"All right, Son. Don't worry. Gus'll feed her, morning and night, as long as she's . . ."

"As long as I can't do it," finished Ken happily.

The doctor put the thermometer in his mouth and told him to keep it shut.

All day Gus went about his work, thinking of Flicka. He had not been back to look at her. He had been given no more orders. If she was alive, the order to shoot her was still in effect. But Kennie was ill; McLaughlin, making his second trip to town, taking the doctor home, would not be back till long after dark.

After their supper in the bunkhouse, Gus and Tim walked down to the brook. They did not speak as they approached the filly, lying stretched out flat on the grassy bank, but their eyes were straining at her to see if she was dead or alive.

She raised her head as they reached her.

"By the powers!" exclaimed Tim; "there she is!"

She dropped her head, raised it again, and moved her legs and became tense as if struggling to rise. But to do so she must use her right hind leg to brace herself against the earth. That was the damaged leg, and at the first bit of pressure with it, she gave up and fell back.

"We'll swing her onto the other side," said Tim. "Then she can help herself."

"Ja. . . ."

Standing behind her, they leaned over, grabbed hold of her left legs, front and back, and gently hauled her over. Flicka was as lax and willing as a puppy. But the moment she found herself lying on her right side, she began to scramble, braced herself with her good left leg, and tried to rise.

"Yee whiz!" said Gus. "She got plenty strength yet."

"Hi!" cheered Tim. "She's up!"

But Flicka wavered, slid down again, and lay flat. This time she gave notice that she would not try again by heaving a deep sigh and closing her eyes.

Gus took his pipe out of his mouth and thought it over. Orders or no orders, he would try to save the filly. Ken had gone too far to be let down.

"Ay'm goin' to rig a blanket sling fur her, Tim, and get her on her feet and keep her up."

There was bright moonlight to work by. They brought down the posthole digger and set two aspen poles deep into the ground on either side of the filly, then, with ropes attached to the blanket, hoisted her by a pulley.

Not at all disconcerted, she rested comfortably in the blanket under her belly, touched her feet on the ground, and reached for the bucket of water Gus held for her.

Kennie was sick a long time. He nearly died. But Flicka picked up. Every day Gus passed the word to Nell, who carried it to Ken. "She's cleaning up her oats. . . . She's out of the sling. . . . She bears a little weight on the bad leg."

Tim declared it was a real miracle. They argued about it, eating their supper.

"Na," said Gus. "It was de cold water, washin' de fever outa her. And more dan dot—it was Ken—you tink it don't count? All night dot boy sits dere and says, 'Hold on, Flicka, Ay'm here wid you. Ay'm standin' by, two of us togedder.' . . ."

Tim stared at Gus without answering, while he thought it over. In the silence, a coyote yapped far off on the plains, and the wind made a rushing sound high up in the jack pines on the hill.

Gus filled his pipe.

"Sure," said Tim finally. "Sure, that's it."

Then came the day when Rob McLaughlin stood smiling at the foot of Kennie's bed and said, "Listen! Hear your friend?"

Ken listened and heard Flicka's high, eager whinny.

"She don't spend much time by the brook any more. She's up at the gate of the corral half the time, nickering for you."

"For me!"

Rob wrapped a blanket around the boy and carried him out to the corral gate.

Kennie gazed at Flicka. There was a look of marveling in his eyes. He felt as if he had been living in a world where everything was dreadful and hurting but awfully real; and *this* couldn't be real; this was all soft and happy, nothing to struggle over or worry about or fight for any more. Even his father was proud of him! He could feel it in the way Rob's big arms held him. It was all like a dream and far away. He couldn't, yet, get close to anything.

But Flicka—Flicka—alive, well, pressing up to him, recognizing him, nickering . . .

Kennie put out a hand—weak and white—and laid it on her face. His thin little fingers straightened her forelock the way he used to do, while Rob looked at the two with a strange expression about his mouth and a glow in his eyes that was not often there.

"She's still poor, Dad, but she's on four legs now."

"She's picking up."

Ken turned his face up, suddenly remembering. "Dad! She did get gentled, didn't she?"

"Gentle—as—a kitten. . . ."

They put a cot down by the brook for Ken, and boy and filly got well together.

■ ■ ■

Early in Bearstone, *Cloyd gives himself a secret name: "Lone Bear." Why do names matter? What thoughts about your own name come to mind as you read?*

The Name Game

from A Book About Names

Milton Meltzer

"Must a name mean something?" Alice asked doubtfully.
"Of course it must," Humpty Dumpty said. . . .
"My name means the shape I am. . . . With a name like yours,
you might be any shape, almost."

Names are symbols. So are most other words. But what names symbolize is unique. A hundred other people may have borne your name, but none of them was just like you. Who else could have had your past, your hopes, your fears, your joys, your sorrows? So the name you carry means something special, something particular, something that is *you*. It makes you aware of yourself as somebody different from everyone else. A name—your name—is a symbol more powerful than any other word.

Whatever your given name, it has a cultural meaning that affects the image other people form of you as the bearer of that name. How you feel about your own name may shape your personality in a positive or negative way. Your parents, or whoever named you, revealed the nature of their interests and concerns and the frame of their culture by their choice of the name they gave you.

There has long been a widespread belief in the power of names. When a name changes, some say, the person changes.

Take the true story of Saul Kurzweil. He was a child in Eastern Europe when an epidemic struck his village and he fell seriously ill. To deceive the Angel of Death, Saul's mother carried him to the synagogue and there had her son renamed Chaim, meaning "life." It fooled the Angel, and Saul recovered.

On the other hand, some thought sickness could be caused by a name. Among certain American Indians and the people of Tibet it was believed that names that did not fit the person could bring on illness. The cure was to take a new name that would fit better. And in ancient times Chinese doctors would write a patient's name on a piece of paper, then burn the paper and mix the ashes with medicine to guarantee that the medicine would cure the sick person.

Inseparable from a name's meaning and power is its sound. "You can love a name," said Gertrude Stein, "and if you love a name, then saying that name any number of times can only make you love it more." Poetry, she added, is "really loving the name of anything."

The study of names (the scholars call it onomastics) has produced a considerable bibliography, which I have freely and gratefully drawn upon. The references venture into history, psychology, anthropology, sociology, linguistics. The many paths into the realm of names and naming are worth pursuing. But what follows is a sample for the casual reader of the pleasures to be found in what the serious students have unearthed.

In Africa

In Africa, the naming ceremonies for black children are fairly consistent throughout the continent. Taken into consideration are the time of day the child is born, the day of the week, and, frequently, special circumstances linked to the child, its parents, its extended family, and the community. To show their happiness at the birth, parents often give names meaning "rejoice," "we are blessed," "luck," "gift of God." Some African names, such as Rain, reflect what happened at the time of birth. Not until the child has been named is it considered a person (perhaps because of the high infant mortality in some places). The final naming is thus seen to complete the act of birth. Many Africans believe it is only the body that dies; the spirit lives on, dwelling in many bodies in many lifetimes.

So You Changed Your Name?

Most African names are single words or a few words shaped into a phrase in the language of the family. For instance, the Yoruba male and female name Ayo means "joy," while the girl's name Ayodele means "joy enters the home." But beyond that first given name, Africans adopt or are given other names, too, so that someone you knew by a particular name some years ago might have an altogether different name when you meet him today. The advertisements in African newspapers frequently carry announcements of people who have changed their personal names or their surnames. Children born of the same parents may have quite different names, because in many African societies family names do not exist.

The Name-Giver

The ancient tribal tradition of the Delaware Indians of Oklahoma bestowed the function of name-giving on those individuals blessed with visions inspired by the Creator. The visionaries were gifted people with powers ordinary people did not have. They were able to give names to their own children and the children of others. Those who were not gifted with visions—the great majority—could confer nick-names on their children, but not real names. Such nicknames were used in everyday exchanges among tribal members. But the real personal name was the mark of identity by which the Creator and his Spirit Forces knew the individual. Some Delawares would never reveal their real name beyond the immediate family. In the hands of one capable of conjuring evil, a person's real name might do him harm, causing disability, blindness, and even death. Such sorcery or witchcraft could not happen with a nickname. The name-giver did not name a newly born baby. The parents would wait until they were reasonably sure the Creator meant the child to remain permanently in the family. Meanwhile, the baby went by a nickname, and at the right time, got the real name from a visionary.

Rawautoaqvaywoaky

Very few of the names originally borne by American Indians, or Native Americans, have been kept unchanged. As far back as scholars have been able to go, they have found nothing that could be called fixed surnames. The Indian names in use when whites first arrived proved very difficult for the early colonists to grasp or pronounce. Among the few recorded in the late 1600s were Abozaweramud, Kekroppamont, and Rawautoaqvaywoaky. When Indians were forced onto reservations, the children and adults who entered government schools or hospitals were given American-style names. The Indians' own names were translated, which accounts for the surnames now familiar to us. These names were linked to personal characteristics (Black Eye, Yellow Boy), or to some bird or animal (Fast Horse, Flying Hawk, Red Owl), or to an aspect of the landscape (Red Cedar, Howling Water, High Pine).

■ ■ ■

Will Hobbs

■ (born in 1947) ■

As a child, Will Hobbs hated to see his family leave their home in the beautiful Alaskan wilderness for life in California. "I remember the beauty of the river and the mountains, the feeling of the place becoming a part of me," he recalls. "I remember when the ship pulled out as we were leaving Alaska, I was standing at the stern and watching the mountains recede, and the tears were streaming down my face."

At his new home, Hobbs remained interested in nature. He explored the San Francisco hills, catching lizards in a noose made from a piece of grass. He never harmed or kept the creatures, however; it was strictly catch and release.

When he grew older, Hobbs hiked and backpacked in many regions of the United States. As a teenager, he worked as a guide and camp director at Philmont Scout Ranch in New Mexico. In 1973, he and his wife Jean moved to southwestern Colorado, where they could enjoy the San Juan Mountains. Today, he and his wife Jean share their love for the wilderness with their nieces and nephews—going on backpacking trips, river journeys, and other explorations of the Southwest.

Hobbs loves nature, but he also loves writing. Even in high school, in fact, he dreamed of becoming an author. At Stanford University, he studied literature to prepare for a career as a writer. After completing his master's degree in 1971, however, Hobbs decided to become an English and reading teacher. He enjoyed teaching junior high and high school students; however, as the years passed, he felt that something was missing from his life.

At the age of thirty-three, Hobbs decided to see if he really could be a writer. A grizzly bear had been killed recently in the San Juan Mountains, but grizzly bears were supposed to be extinct in Colorado. This real-life incident became the "seed" for

Bearstone. Will also drew much of the material for the novel from his own experiences. "The Pride of the West" gold mine, for example, is based on fact: A friend of Hobbs's owned a closed-down mine with that name. The friend had talked about reopening the mine, and that gave Hobbs the idea for the character of Walter Landis. "I thought his chances were slim in real life," Hobbs has commented, "so why not have a go at making it happen in a story?" Hobbs moved his friend's mine about a hundred miles to the upper Pine River. Next, he created Cloyd Atcitty, the Ute boy, to help and befriend Walter. The character of Cloyd is based on a student that his wife had taught. Even the descriptions of ranching come from Hobbs's experiences helping a friend bring in the hay in the summer.

Still, the writing of *Bearstone* did not go smoothly. Early versions of the book were not what publishers wanted. After several rejection letters and only rare encouragement, Hobbs attended a writer's workshop in Aspen, Colorado. There, writer Russell Banks helped him refine his ideas. It took six versions of the book and eight years of work, however, before *Bearstone* finally was accepted for publication.

Today, Hobbs is a full-time writer. He urges his readers to take an interest in the natural world. He also encourages those who are interested in becoming writers to read: "For me and for almost all writers, it's reading that primes the pump for writing. . . . Writing is sinking a well. If you're a reader you can sink a well just about anywhere and find good water . . . if you're willing to work at it."